THE BLUEPRINT TO ENDING
ABORTION
IN THE CHURCH

PASTORS AND CHURCH LEADERS HANDBOOK FOR ADDRESSING THE MOST PRESSING ISSUE IN THE PEW

MIKE GOSS

ISBN: 979-8-89504-134-5

TABLE of CONTENTS

PREFACE

First Chronicles (12:32) tells us that the men of Issachar understood the times, so they knew what action should be taken to lead Israel in the right direction. Every generation faces its own unique challenge. No previous generation of God's anointed has ever been tasked with restoring reverence for human life.

This book is written to assist those in pastoral leadership to gain a comprehensive understanding of the life issue to shepherd God's people through an unprecedented time of moral and ethical challenges. It's critical to speak with clarity and compassion from a theological and a practical perspective, on the most explosive and polarizing societal issue the church has faced since the abolition of slavery.

It's impossible to deny that believers are drowning in a sea of misperception, ignorance, and defiance—being caught in the undertow of abortion rights propaganda instigated by the Adversary of our soul. They're floundering because of a lack of knowledge.

This project is long overdue. In 2015, Lifeway Research, commissioned by Care Net, a network of over 1,200 pregnancy resource centers, conducted a study on Protestant and Catholic women who had an abortion and their views on the church. It exposed a significant and troubling issue inside the church walls. The most troubling discovery for church leadership, aside from the surprisingly large number of women having abortions, is that women facing unplanned pregnancies feel they must seek solutions beyond the church.

Research shows 54% of women who identified themselves as Christian were in regular church attendance when they had their first abortion.

Question: If a woman in your congregation were struggling with a complicated pregnancy, would she know who she could reach out to for help? Could she or does she know if she could come to you? If she did, how would you direct her? According to the study 16% of pastors either referred, drove, paid for, or encouraged the woman to have an abortion. Only 40% of respondents agreed that it was safe to talk to a pastor about abortion. Only 40% agreed that pastors are sensitive to the pressures a woman faces with an unplanned pregnancy. Of the respondents, 76% said the church had zero influence on their decision to terminate their pregnancy. And half of the women who had an abortion said their pastors' teaching on forgiveness don't seem to apply to terminated pregnancies.

Far too many wrong answers have been given. What will make abortion an unnecessary option in your congregation while saving the life of a child and the mother from possibly decades of shame and regret.

Let's assume these women had a strong belief that abortion goes against their Christian values, but felt compelled to go through with it due to their circumstances. Suppose 60-76% of them believed the church couldn't help them. Is it fair to conclude that we bear some responsibility for the loss of the 60 million human lives, along with society's moral indifference toward unborn life? I believe the time has come for an honest examination of our role in allowing fifty years of abortion rights evangelism to win over hearts of our people while we remain silent.

The good news is that many in the church who are "Pro-Choice" do so based on circumstance rather than conviction. This indicates that they are not necessarily pro-abortion. Instead, it reveals a hope or at least a willingness to see how the church may be able to help them overcome perceived insurmountable barriers, which is causing them to consider abortion as their best option.

Before I get into the solution, I felt it was necessary to devote time to giving you a fuller understanding of the depth and scope of the problem. Despite the abortion rights claim that abortion empowers women, you'll discover the harmful affect "her body, her choice" rhetoric has had and is having on women. And not just women, but the fathers of the unborn child, and the church. And obviously the unborn child.

You'll see why I say as God-honoring as our Pro-Life mission has been, this *Blueprint* shows that despite our sincere efforts, we've fallen short. We must go beyond just being Pro-Life to becoming Pro-Abundant Life if we're going to break the cycle of intergenerational abortion.

The abortion rights evangelist sees women facing a complicated pregnancy decision as mere customers who require abortion as the solution, ignoring the underlying reasons that led them to seek such a drastic solution. They disregard the underlying factors that compel one-third of them to seek such a drastic solution again.

Contrast that with Jesus's ministry model, where every encounter was meant to be transformational and aimed at addressing their spiritual needs. He emphasized coming as you are, but don't stay as you came. Whether it was the woman at the well or the one caught in the act of adultery, he recognized their deeper spiritual needs were far too great to be ignored. Certainly, having an abortion terminates an unwanted pregnancy, but it does not address the underlying factors.

I see this as a blueprint primarily because it outlines a coherent and compelling strategy for ending abortion in church, or at least being viewed as an unnecessary option. It's based on the most well-known unexpected pregnancy (from a human perspective) the world has ever known. And if followed will spare so many women from the regret of abortion and preborn babies from a premature death. At the very least I'm thankful for its ability to open blind eyes of those who think that abortion is the correct solution.

The Pro-Choice evangelist is not equipped to address unplanned pregnancies in a way that does not leave wounded and dead souls behind. Nor do they have a desire to. The church, though, has been called and equipped. Peter wrote in his first Epistle (1:3) that God has equipped us with everything we need for life and godliness. All that's needed is for the church to be the church. The following pages prove that we have everything we need to offer including compassionate help and hope to those facing difficult pregnancy decisions. My prayer is God will be able to commend us one day as he did the men of Issachar for understanding the challenges and the opportunities of our time, to lead His people in the right direction, and the moral will to do it. May God bless our efforts.

———————————————————————————————————

ACKNOWLEDGMENTS

In memory of the Reverend J.R. Goss

I believe there's an unidentifiable force that beats beneath the breastplate of every male child that expresses itself in the desire to make his father proud. That force beats in me every day of my life.

To my wife, Wanda

God's greatest gift to me. Thank you for four-plus decades of unwavering love and support, which, after all these years, continues to motivate me to try harder.

To Courtney and Jonathan

I am incredibly proud of the remarkable individuals you are becoming. Your determination, resiliency, and kindness toward others are inspiring. I am excited to see all the incredible things you will continue to achieve. You have enriched my life in countless ways and I am honored to be your father.

To Roland

Thank you! Thank you for your generous investment of time almost three years ago in a total stranger. This work would not have been possible without your willingness to share your uncommon insights. I've often felt that your name should have been included as a co-author because it was impossible to credit you for every line I wrote or insight I've extracted from your keen intellect. Your relentless pursuit of protecting the unborn and the well-being of women and men has been and continues to be instrumental in shaping the direction and depth of this ministry.

INTRODUCTION

Now that the decades-long nightmare is over, it's still difficult to understand how something so harmful to women, innocent infants, the fathers of those infants, families, the church, and the community at large, is so vigorously defended and in stark opposition to the Creator of life. Even with the advent of 4D ultrasound technology, fetal heartbeat monitors, and stories of babies surviving at less than four months, the majority still oppose their right to life.

As a Black man, I cannot escape the connection between the dehumanization of chattel slavery and the dehumanization of preborn babies. As many times as I've seen them, I'm still unable to look at pictures of overflowing crowds of white people with kids in tow, all dressed in their Sunday best, being entertained by a black man being shamelessly humiliated and then hung from a tree without feeling the slow boil of anger. I'm unable to comprehend how their minds could be so dark to not feel a twinge of guilt or compassion. The only way possible they could impose such inhumane treatment upon us was if they did not see our shared humanity. They were killing a human with feelings and emotions just like them. They had contorted their thinking that they were not killing a human like themselves, created in the image of God.

Likewise, it's difficult for me to comprehend how 78% of Americans believe it is a woman's right to end the life of a healthy baby, without feeling for the unborn baby the way I feel looking at my brothers being tortured. Perhaps they can't empathize with the pain an infant must feel having a long hypodermic needle being jabbed in the base of the skull, and then torn into so many pieces when pulled through the birth canal that it required an inventory of body parts to make sure none were left behind. Or what the infants must feel as they thrash about fighting for their life, trying to escape being scaled to death from a powerful saline solution. A solution so strong that when they came out it had turned their skin was a cherry red. And the latest method where they're starved to death by means of a chemical abortion. Some states have even codified into law the Born Alive Act, whereby the grace of God, if a baby miraculously survives a botched abortion, he or she is to be allowed to die while trained medical professionals stand by, because it's the mothers' will. My God! What have we done to ourselves?

I believe centuries from now, if the Lord tarries, students in history classes will ask in disbelief, "You mean there was once a law declaring that a woman had a right to end the life of her baby, even up until the day of delivery if she chose?" Followed by, "But why? How could they think that was right? They were human just like them."

Finally, the Supreme Court reversed itself, ruling that a woman did not have that constitutional right. Now, if only they had the power to reverse the societal ills that resulted from five decades of what amounts to a vicious backhand in the face of the Life Giver himself.

As it turns out, we flipped open the lid on a Pandora's Box of issues that perverted our priorities, making the right to choose supreme over life itself. In doing so, we set free a deadly, multi-headed, sin-breathing monster, blowing out a host of untamable societal ills that we'll never force back into the box. Proverbs warned us long ago that there was a way that seemed right but ultimately led to a destructive end.

The only difference is, this never seemed right. And it wasn't. Sixty million lives have been trashed as millions and millions of women and men are lugging around shame and regret in silence. A society that no longer has a reverence for life inside the womb or outside, confirms that it wasn't right.

We can't bring back the millions of lives lost. We can't undo the hurt millions of lives experienced. And although the courts can make abortion illegal, only God, through his church, can make it unnecessary. This book shows us why and how. I've identified five critical needs that must be addressed that will render the need for abortion to be an unnecessary option within the church.

I Was Blind But . . .

I'm ashamed. I have not always recognized the sanctity of preborn life. I have not always considered their lives equal to mine, or my wife or my children, my parents, my friends, or even strangers. I haven't always been able to see we have our shared humanity. I was blind. Looking back I cared about an unborn child losing its life, as I did for a blackbird losing its. It still agitates my conscience to admit this, but when I reflect on my younger years, I was guilty of, albeit unconsciously, racist bigotry toward unborn black babies. I believed a particular preborn life should be put down like a lame horse. In certain familial circumstances, I thought it was in the best interest of all if their lives were terminated. The sad truth is I wasn't in the classroom by myself. I remember an acquaintance essentially saying that some babies are better off being put to death. Although he didn't say it in those exact words, the meaning was clear. Those demented and discriminating thoughts would have never found a safe harbor in our hearts if we somehow had a way of knowing that the babies we condemned would one day sit on the Supreme Court of the United States. Or would become the next great black scientist in the mold of G W. Carver. Or would they one day unlock the secrets to the long-sought-after cure for breast cancer? Or the next Martin Luther King, who awakened the lifeless conscience of our nation by insisting that racial equality was in the best interests of white people, as it was ours.

I'm ashamed to admit that while looking down on others for being born into a less-than-ideal family structure, I was the kettle calling the pot black. I came into the world under those same dismal family conditions—both parents were poor, uneducated, and unmarried. There was no commitment to each other or me which led to me living in five different households before age ten. I should have understood the need for compassion better than anyone. However, by the standards I measured others by, my life should have ended in a watery grave, never seeing the light of day. I had sight, but I lacked insight to see terminating a child's life was not an act of love or compassion for the child or the mother. I was a spiritual cripple limping along in the dark.

One of the reasons abortions permeate our pews and are endorsed by Christians is because they are filled with those who are blind like I was. They hold an unconscious bias against poor preborn life, as I did. I forgot where I started now that I lived in a nicer house, drove a nicer car, and dined out as often as I dined in. My credit card statement revealed that almost every dollar was filed under the me, myself, and I category. Although I attended weekly worship and joined in singing *Our God is an Awesome God*, privately, I believed that the life of a child born into poverty is beyond the reach of a loving God. Rather than having that liability hanging over our heads, I believed it was more cost-effective to sacrifice their lives on the altar of economic savings while they're still in the womb rather than face the probability of funding what I saw as endless social programs.

Abortion was the first and only option I felt appropriate for a young mother who's already living on the margins of life, with limited education, limited job prospects, and struggling from day to day. In my mind, she was a hopeless liability. I could not see her through eyes of compassion as Christ saw me—someone with a need to come into a transforming relationship with him.

My flippant and unsympathetic attitudes toward our less fortunate preborn brothers and sisters served as a public barometer for my privately held beliefs. As they struggled at the bottom of America's melting pot, my disregard for their plight enabled the heat to be turned up. Not because of hate. Not because of skin color. Because they weren't a member of my social class, the Hindus refer to as a caste system. Classism has always been a form of Jim Crowism. Just as reprehensible as racism. It turned me, of all people, into a social segregationist. Unknowingly, I was forcing those who were not in my class to give up their seats to choose birth and move to the back of the bus and stand in the section marked inferiority, so I could take a seat in support of legislation that equated to social injustice for them and their unborn babies. I was blind then, but now I see.

CHAPTER 2

An Impassioned Plea
to Pro-Choice Pastors

I admit that this chapter has been quite challenging. As a result, I ended up procrastinating for as long as I could. My struggle is amplified by my respect for God's under-shepherd and the task of delivering a somewhat pointed message in a way that will ignite your mind without scorching your soul. No one was more skilled at that than Jesus, the master of the parables. But even he, at times, would toss that approach and go straight to the heart of the matter, such as in John 6 when he wanted to make sure his followers understood the cost of discipleship. His words ignited their minds and set their souls on fire, and all but the most committed walked away, complaining it was too much to accept.

Certainly, depending on where you stand on the life issue, some of what you're about to read will leave you feeling like those who walked away. *These are hard truths. Many will find them difficult to accept.* As you read, please keep in mind my impassioned plea is not meant to offend but to enlighten. It's not meant to condemn but to motivate.

My former pastor, the late Dr. A. Louis Patterson, used to say, "Satan carries a slippery shoe, and if you're not careful, he'll slip it on you." After the overturning of abortion rights so that women no longer had a constitutional right to terminate the life of their perfectly normal baby, 50 years of non-stop Pro-Choice propaganda had influenced the entire culture, including many of those who identify as ambassadors of Christ. To be salt and light to a dark and dying world were standing on the same side of the fence as atheists. Even the likes of Pontius Pilate would consider it high treason against our King. The patron Saint, Mother Teresa, said, "If abortion is not a sin, nothing is a sin."

Logically thinking, these "ambassadors" must have concluded in their hearts that each time a child is aborted, the angels are gathered around the throne of God, not weeping but rejoicing. That the child God knew before He purposefully knitted them together in their mother's womb, mapping out all the days of their life have been intentionally and violently cut short, somehow brings him Glory. That in God's eyes there's no distinction between abortion and birth. Logically thinking.

Before preaching the doctrine of *it's her body, her choice,* the Pro-Choice man or woman of God *must* understand that they're about to lob a psychological hand grenade right into the middle of the congregation where so many have already been left carrying shame from an abortion or supporting someone who has. Before you lob that grenade, allow me to show you who's about to get blown up by "her body, her choice."

As you look around, you may notice people sitting silently with an unresponsive and expressionless look. No one applauds or is shouting in amen. Preach it! And for a good reason. Many of these people have fought with all their might to bury the shame deep within and forget about it. Some are still trying to do so. Society may have approved that it was a woman's right to sacrifice her child, but every mother's spiritual DNA carries the inner knowledge that it wasn't a life that should have been sacrificed. Instead, it was a life she should have been willing to sacrifice for. She was manipulated into believing that the unborn child was part of her body, which, for many, led to irreversible feelings of shame and regret. Does it mean now, hearing her spiritual leader proclaim it was her body, her choice, that her repentance was in vain? Not according to scripture. And no pastor, church counselor, church mother, or anyone else will convince her otherwise. Pastors; many are still hurting! Listen to this:

I don't want to hear it was my choice. I know it was my choice and I regret that choice. The last thing I need to hear from the pastor is something he knows it, and I know it was wrong. What I needed most at that moment was someone calling me to a higher standard. Not someone lowering the bar. And assuring me it was not the end of the world as I thought. And they were going to help me get through it. I'm not blaming anybody but myself. My abortion was on December 7th, 1992. I can still remember the thump of her heartbeat. I haven't been able to forgive myself for it.
- Anonymous

The saddest part of her story, one of many I've heard, is that she has never been able to experience the liberation from the consequences of sin that is available to all who ask. She can't ask because, in her mind, she doesn't feel she deserves to be forgiven. There is no other area where there is more collective brokenness than this.

A young man is singing in the choir behind you who is still angry because, in his words, "she killed my baby." Is his anger misplaced? If you look out in the far back left corner on the last row, there's a young woman at that very moment wrestling with the decision to terminate the life of her baby.

Have you green-lighted her decision even though she knows it's a grave sin? Her conscience reveals it is sin against God. Her choice to disregard God's truth in relationships has led her to this regrettable crossroads.. Is she perceiving her pastor's subtle suggestion to mask one sin with another?

On the back row of that same pew, on the other end, is a young man who's waffling in his decision to support his pregnant girlfriend. Is this just the word he needed to hear from the one he considers his spiritual leader to wash his hands of the entire situation and free himself of his impending responsibility? And should she decide to give birth, will he use the pastor's words to throw it back in her face? "After it all was your choice. Even Pastor said it. Now live with it!" No one wants to live with the consequences of our poor choices, so whenever possible we force it off on those with no choice.

Then there's the father who confided in me that on the way home from church one Sunday, he found himself struggling to explain to their fifteen-year-old daughter the Pastor's Pro-Choice position. He said he struggled to explain their family's biblical worldview that they taught in their home, in a way that didn't contradict the pastor.

Let's not forget about the would-be grandparents who always sit up front. There's a hollow place in their heart that no one knows about but them. It's the place where the love of a grandchild should have been had it not been for the pernicious role her body, her choice ideology played, robbing them of their one chance to become grandparents. You hit them, too, pastor. Sitting directly behind them happens to be a woman who doesn't care how adamant her pastor is about a woman's right to terminate the life of her child.

She's not doing that a third time. Period! There's a childless sister behind her who aborted the only child she had and has never been able to conceive, wondering if it's God's way of punishing her. Across from her is a guy; he's single, in his 50s, and fatherless. He carries regret for pressuring his then-girlfriend to terminate the only child he has ever had. The walking wounded from the emotional fall-out from this Demonic doctrine of 'your body, your choice', are scattered all over the sanctuary.

Many church members find themselves straddling the fence. Uncertain about which side to come down on. They are constantly being pulled on by the media, political leaders, celebrities, and everyday people they encounter. All pulling against the moral witness that beats within their chest, reminding them this is wrong! Despite this confusion, they hold on to the belief that the sanctity of human life is a central tenet of their faith. As far back as Sunday school, they were taught that we're created in the image of God. In that Sunday school class, they were also taught that their bodies were not their own but bought by the brutal death of Christ. They long for a clear, authoritative voice based on scripture to help them navigate the confusion and misunderstandings surrounding this issue.

Although the pews are filled with people carrying guilt or shame from having had an abortion or having aided and abetted one, are they really comfortable having their pastor condone a practice where the only people in the Bible who approved the death of infants were Pharaoh and Herod? Both evil men wielded their power to sacrifice the defenseless for convenience.

The doctrine of her body, her choice gives women the

illusion that she's in the driver's seat of their life. She doesn't need to answer to God or anyone else. Not even the father of the child. But more damaging than all the previously mentioned reasons is that it blasphemes the character of God. It encourages total irreverence for the capabilities of the Great I Am. Insinuating that God is not able to make *all* things come together for good when our backs are up against the wall. That he's not omnipotent but impotent. And he's too powerless, untrustworthy, and uncaring for her to place all her hope in Him at a time when so much is at stake.

There's another compelling reason for my pleading with the Pro-Choice pastors to reconsider their position. In Deuteronomy 30:19 we see Pastor Moses passionately imploring his people "I call the heavens and the earth as witnesses against you that I have set before you, (you can't say I didn't warn you) life and death, blessings and curses. Now, (please) choose life so that you and your children may live" (emphasis added). This passage reveals the sincere heart of this Man of God who's deeply concerned about the ramifications of wrong choices by those under his care. And wants to discharge his responsibility to them and to God by making sure they know what's at stake.

Now contrast that with, "It's your choice," implying "fine if you do, fine if you don't. I'm leaving it up to you. If you choose death and curses for you and your children, it's no skin off my back." What pastor would tell his congregation, "Fine by me if you want to go to hell? It's your body it's your choice." Knowing full well the promises of hell, we know that pastor would surely be dealt with.

Would not the pastor, knowing death, await those they tell it's their choice if they want to terminate the life of their child not be disciplined to the same extent? We don't hear, "it's their choice" at the invitation. Nor do we hear "it's your choice" at offering time. So why now since the promise of death and curses awaits them and their children?

In Pro-Life work, we witness this promise being fulfilled through intergenerational death caused by abortion. The grandmother kicked it off, her daughter followed suit, and her daughter after that. Three generations! The word of God will not return void. Here's the hard part: forgive me in advance for asking this if it offends you. My only intent is to cause someone to think long and hard about their Pro-Choice position. Would I be off base and theologically wrong to suggest that the blood of these babies aborted by their mothers will one day come pouring back to the Pro-Choice pastor's door. Although it was an open book test with the correct answer already given, they led them to believe they didn't care that they were choosing death when they told them "it's their choice."

I end my impassioned plea to please understand the gravity of your words. A child's life is at stake, along with a woman's emotional health. I plead with you to delve deeper into the complexities surrounding the issue of abortion. I believe you will find compelling evidence that calls for urgent action to help alleviate the problem with solutions that honor God. Pregnancy care ministries are a good place to start so those facing difficult pregnancy decisions turn to their church for support, rather than resorting to an abortion clinic.

CHAPTER 3

Her Body Her Choice. At What Cost?

If there was ever a catchphrase that proved to hurt more than it helped those it was meant to serve, "my body, my choice," is it. This singular phrase has been mindlessly repeated for nearly fifty years to the point they've been able to even convince some Christians that opposition to abortion is based on a desire to control women.

No one asks if our opposition to a woman running across a busy interstate in rush hour traffic with her baby in her arms be based on a desire to control her. The reality is that opposition to abortion is motivated by compassion—compassion for her and especially her unborn child. A woman who finds herself in such dire straits that she feels her only choice is to take the life of her unborn baby needs compassion and not judgment.

The Pro-Choice community advocates for freedom of choice, but do we really have complete control over our bodies? We don't have the choice to take illegal substances like crystal meth, as laws are in place to prevent us from doing so. Consider a scenario where someone chops off one of their fingers with a hatchet, and then repeats it the following five days. If someone intervenes to stop the person, she argues that it's her body and she has the right to do what she wants with it. As a civilized society, we consider those types of behaviors even though it's her body. Similarly, in a civilized society, a woman does not have unlimited control over her body, let alone the body of a baby growing inside her.

When examining the available data on abortions in the United States, it becomes clear that the circumstances that led to a woman's unplanned pregnancy and subsequent abortion can continue to affect her long after the procedure is over. According to a study on the psychological effects of abortion, as many as 20% of women experience regret, depression, and other emotional and psychological reactions after an abortion. With approximately one million abortions taking place in the US every year, this means that around 200,000 women may suffer psychological harm each year. Over the past 50 years, this amounts to approximately 10 million women who may have been affected by the emotional and psychological aftermath of having an abortion.

Another cost of "my body, my choice" is women who faced difficult pregnancy decisions who were often left without the necessary support to consider the long-term effects of their choices. Although abortion may seem like a quick solution, it doesn't address the underlying issues of poverty, sexual abuse, or relationship problems that put the woman at risk of needing an abortion. As Christian leaders, it's important to provide women with comprehensive care and resources that address all aspects of their situation to help them make God-honoring decisions.

Legalized abortion has a significant but less discussed impact on the family structure. It led to the separation of the family from the moment the child was in the womb. The legalization of abortion allowed motherhood to begin at conception, but fatherhood was not recognized until birth. This separation, like pulling a loose thread, began unraveling the first institution created by God paving the way for the "my body, my choice" rhetoric. Clearly, the Supreme Court overstepped its boundaries when it granted women the sole decision-making authority, disregarding the effects it would have on others, especially the father and the unborn child.

"My body, my choice", encourages women to go it alone. This self-isolation comes at the worst possible time, leading her down a path where the only option she's able to see is abortion. This feeling of isolation can be overwhelming, with many women feeling abortion is the only solution.

Millions of abortion-minded women who felt that isolation, are thankful today for the sonogram bill that was first introduced in Texas. And so are their children who were spared because of it. The bill required a waiting period and a sonogram to give pregnant women more information before making their decision. Before the widespread use of sonogram bills, many pregnant women who were unsure about their next step would visit abortion clinics for pregnancy confirmation. However, after seeing their unborn child through the sonogram, 90% of these women changed their minds and decided not to go through with it. This highlights how some women's fears can be exploited in such situations, leading them to make decisions that they may later regret.

While "my body, my choice" may have liberated some women, it liberated some men too. It allowed men who were already looking for a way of escape to slip out a back door since the law stated that they had no rights and thus no responsibilities. This withdrawal further isolated the woman who is now facing the biggest decision of her life—one that will stay with her forever.

This places the abortion-vulnerable woman at even

greater risk. The most common reason women give for the need to terminate their pregnancy is the lack of their partner's emotional and financial support. The only place left for her to turn now is the worst place, an abortion provider, where they stand ready with a well-rehearsed list of reasons to prevent her from seeing beyond the immediacy of her situation.

While it liberated some men, it alienated others. Men who were ready and willing to take on the full responsibility for their unborn child are left with feelings of helplessness and hopelessness because the court says it's the woman's body and, therefore, her choice alone.

From a societal standpoint, the highest cost of "my body, my choice" is it has decimated the nuclear family structure of a father, mother, and child. This shift began with the promotion of abortion as the solution to reduce out-of-wedlock births. However, the opposite has occurred. Abortions have skyrocketed, and out-of-wedlock births have skyrocketed. The cost of additional social programs needed to support single mother-led households, which are often the poorest in the nation, is being borne by taxpayers. It is important to note that almost every tax dollar spent on social programs can be linked to the breakdown of the nuclear family. It's clear that we owe women, men, and ourselves the better way outlined in the *Blueprint* that addresses the high cost of this satanic inspired "my body my choice." How men really feel about abortion shows further the depth of deception.

CHAPTER 4

Reproductive Rights: Just Another "Red Herring"

Throughout history, various red herrings have been used to manipulate public opinion, shape policy, and divert attention from pressing societal issues. They are a common tool for defense attorneys trying to confuse the jury from the central issue. In warfare, they're used as decoys to conceal movement to destroy the enemy.

"Red herring" is a figurative term for a strategy that distracts from the issue at hand. The term reproductive rights is one of abortion rights' most successful strategies. They're using it to manipulate public opinion by diverting attention from an unethical and immoral agenda that seeks to wield power over vulnerable populations.

In any other area rights are defined as the ability or inability to exercise what a specific right would guarantee. For instance, the right to free speech concerns one's capacity to speak or refrain from speaking. The right to vote relates to the ability to vote or not vote. Therefore, the definition of reproductive rights must involve the right to reproduce or abstain from reproducing. The act of reproduction occurs at the point of conception, as this is when a new human life is "produced." Consequently, an issue falling under reproductive rights would involve anything that limits an individual's ability to reproduce, such as forced sterilization, or denying access to birth control in an effort to control their reproductive capability.

For example, during the 20th century, eugenics, a pseudoscientific belief in improving the genetic quality of the human population through selective breeding, gained traction in the U.S. Under the guise of eugenics, state governments implemented policies and programs aimed at controlling reproduction in marginalized populations. The most notable case of denial of reproductive rights was where Blacks, particularly Black women, were subjected to sterilization procedures without their consent or full understanding of the implications. They were chosen because they were poor, disabled, or incarcerated and therefore deemed "unfit" or "undesirable" by state authorities. In the state of North Carolina alone, thousands were forcibly sterilized. This is what a denial of reproductive freedom looks like. But no one is arguing against that.

Reproductive rights or freedom as it relates to abortion is not what the abortion debate is about. The abortion debate is about denying someone the ability to kill what is already reproduced or, rather, the "product of conception"—a new, unique human life—a baby. Of course, even the most ardent Pro-Choice supporter would say it is wrong and should be illegal to give someone the right to kill a child outside the womb. The Pro-Life position essentially seeks to align the moral and legal framework about what happens outside the womb to what happens inside the womb.

Now that this smokescreen laid down by the Enemy of our soul has been blown away we see that denying women their reproductive freedom only applies if they're being prevented or restricted in some way from conception.

The term reproductive rights is only one more red herring in a long list that abortion rights advocates use, initiated by our adversary to divert our attention from the real issue: the right to destroy a life that's already in "production." The *Blueprint* is a strategy that the church can use that makes that a worthless "red herring."

CHAPTER 5

The "Great Hypocrisy" of the Pro-Choice Movement

Pro-Choice advocates say they want to take down all barriers that stand between a woman and her freedom to choose what's best for her. But do they really mean what they say? I've even questioned why they don't just come out and say what the facts prove. The facts speak for themselves. I was taught to never go by what they say. Go by what they do.

What Pro-Choice advocates have said for almost 50 years is that they would prefer no woman need an abortion. Classifying abortion as a need is like a nine-year-old telling his dad he needs a new pair of two-hundred-dollar Jordans. Their longstanding position has been that women should be empowered to make their own decisions based on what they feel is best for them, whether that means carrying a pregnancy to term or having an abortion. Therefore, there shouldn't be any obstacles that impede her ability to choose what she believes is the best option for her. And if there are obstacles, they're committed to helping to remove them. That is their official position. But that's not what they do.

It may surprise some, but those of us who are Pro-Life feel the same way. We believe that women should be able to make the choices they feel are best for them. We feel we have a responsibility to help remove obstacles that prevent them from exercising their freedom of choice. As advocates for life though, we do not have a responsibility to remove obstacles to abortion.

On the other hand, Pro-Choice advocates have just as much of a responsibility to remove obstacles to birth as they do for abortion. Their pro "choice" platform prioritizes a woman's right to make her own choices, whether it's to continue a pregnancy or have an abortion. Shouldn't then their very vocal advocacy for access to reproductive healthcare extend to those who need prenatal care and support services, and when their conscience dictates, carry their baby to full term. Yes, it should.

Why doesn't it? It's in line with the principles of reproductive autonomy and bodily sovereignty that they fight tooth and nail when it pertains to the right to have an abortion. They forget about these other women's need for a choice.

These "forgotten" women are the ones who expose the hypocrisy of the Pro-Choice movement. The forgotten women are hundreds of thousands of women each year who terminate their pregnancies because of what they see as insurmountable obstacles and they feel they have no other option than to abort. If Pro-Choice advocates truly do not care what choice a woman makes as long as she has the right to make it, shouldn't their zeal to remove obstacles for the abortion-determined woman also extend to removing obstacles for the abortion-vulnerable woman? If not, the harsh reality is, they're masquerading as Pro-Choice advocates when they are Pro-Choice hypocrites.

CHAPTER 6

Abortion: Offspring of the Sexual Revolution

To understand how we've sunk to a place where we justify this godless sacrificial act where the mother can choose to terminate the life of her child to free her from the impending responsibilities resulting from the unwanted consequences of sex outside of marriage, we must reach back in history to see where it all began. The legalization of abortion is often thought to be the product of a simple Supreme Court decision in 1973.   But this decision was the culmination of a much deeper cultural shift in the country that began long before Roe v. Wade.

The sordid fate for the unborn came on the heels of the "free love" movement, where people rebelled against traditional societal norms that forbade sex outside of marriage and adultery. This movement was a response to the Vietnam War and cultural changes, and it was characterized by a "make love, not war" mentality. As a result, many societal mores that had been passed down for generations were rejected, leading to a sordid fate for the unborn. Hugh Hefner, the creator of the pornographic magazines Playboy and Playgirl, which birthed the idioms" Playas and Playgirls," used it to signify one's pursuit of unlimited sex partners. These popular magazines helped create the country's insatiable appetite for sex outside of marriage.

The possibility of children was a threat to sexual freedom, and the unencumbered sexual lifestyle sought by the sexual revolution. So if a child was born, goodbye sexual freedom. Even though there was the availability of a reliable birth control it wasn't always used, so there remained the possibility of pregnancy. They believed abortion was the perfect solution for their desire for a sexual lifestyle free from the possibility of having children. The sexual revolution's leadership felt they had to advocate for legalized abortion. There could be no "victory" without it.

The Pro-Choice movement framed the abortion issue as a "woman's issue" despite the reality that a woman at risk for an abortion needs the support from the father of the child, her family, her church, and her community. Such reforms were deemed necessary to have complete control over sexual choice and practices.

By deceiving the public into seeing this as merely a woman's issue, the movement sought to silence opposition to abortion by framing it as sexist, and an interference of Christians in the decision between a woman and her doctor. The sexual revolution openly challenged God's design for sex, marriage, and family. This rebellion against the laws of God resulted in severe negative consequences, not only for sixty million unborn children who lost their lives, but for the millions and millions of women and men who ended up forfeiting the very thing they sought—freedom.

Their attempt to free themselves from the laws of God, instead found themselves trapped with years, and often a lifetime, of shame and regret after the decision to terminate the life of their child.

CHAPTER 7

Abortion Pill: The New Battlefield

Now that Roe has been overturned it's easy to think the war over the life of the unborn is over. Not so. The abortion pill has redrawn the battle lines. The abortion industry has long sought to turn abortions into a simple consumer transaction. The abortion pill moves them closer to their goal of aborting a preborn as easy as ordering a meal from Uber Eats. For years abortion rights advocates ran with the slogan "making abortions safe, rare and legal." Now it's abortions anywhere, anytime, do it yourself.

Since the Dobbs decision that led to the overturning of Roe v. Wade, more and more women are now resorting to self-induced abortions using the abortion pill, RU-486. A process that for years was considered necessary to be supervised by medical professionals can now be performed by anyone, even a 12-year-old. Chemical abortion involves a two-drug regimen that can be taken up to 70 days (10 weeks) into the pregnancy with the intention of terminating the pregnancy. The first drug, mifepristone, is taken to block the naturally occurring hormone, progesterone, which is essential to nurture and sustain life. Blocking this hormone essentially deprives the baby of nutrients, leading to its death. After 24-72 hours of taking mifepristone, the second drug, usually misoprostol, is taken to induce labor, causing the uterus to contract and expel the deceased baby.

For some women, a medical abortion may not be an option if it is too far along in their pregnancy. A medical abortion shouldn't be attempted if they're more than nine weeks (after the start of her last period). Some types of medical abortions aren't recommended after seven weeks of pregnancy.

Mifepristone, can pose a serious health risk if a woman currently has an intrauterine device (IUD) and suspects a pregnancy outside of the uterus (known as ectopic pregnancy); and has certain medical conditions such as bleeding disorders, certain heart or blood vessel diseases, severe liver, kidney, or lung disease, an uncontrolled seizure disorder, is taking a blood thinner or certain steroid medicine, or has an allergy to the medicine used. Yet, now they're allowed to become their own physician without any regard for the risks it imposes.

Previously, the FDA required a woman seeking a chemical abortion to see a doctor to ensure she does not have an ectopic pregnancy (i.e., a fertilized egg attached outside the uterus) or another pregnancy-related condition that may result in life-threatening complications. Also, the doctor makes sure the pregnancy is accurately dated, as the abortion pill is authorized for use only 10 weeks after the mother's last period or up to 7 weeks from fertilization. At this stage, the child's heart is beating, lungs are expanding, and all organs are fully developed.

Health risks associated with one of the drugs (mifepristone) are serious enough to warrant a rare safety requirement called a Risk Evaluation and Mitigation Strategy (REMS). According to the FDA, REMS is a drug safety program the FDA can require for certain medications with serious safety concerns to help ensure the benefits of the medication outweigh its risks.

However, these safety protocols are being stripped away to ensure access to "underserved" populations. The abortion pill is dangerous in many ways to all women, and the decision to allow women to administer the medication without medical supervision only adds another layer of risk. Unsurprisingly, failure to comply with safety standards is not unusual. For example, an ectopic pregnancy can only be diagnosed with an ultrasound, a procedure often skipped. In addition, a pregnancy will sometimes be incorrectly dated on purpose to gain access to pills for women farther along in their pregnancies.

With very little or no medical oversight, young women are being caught in unexpected life-threatening situations at home alone. Some are experiencing severe hemorrhaging and having to be rushed to emergency rooms for life-saving medical attention. After taking the pills and thinking they are no longer pregnant some women are surprised after going to a pregnancy resource center for a free ultrasound that their baby survived the abortion attempt and is still alive. This is possibly due to a proliferation of black-market abortion pills easily accessible online. One young woman home alone was further along than she realized and aborted a fully developed three-inch drenched-in blood infant. She took a picture holding it in the palm of her hand not knowing what to do. She placed a distressed call to the pregnancy center inquiring if she should bury the baby somewhere. Her conscience would not allow her to flush her baby down the toilet or throw it out with the trash as some do. Some women are so desperate to end their pregnancy that they take way beyond the recommended two pills.

As preachers of the Gospel, we must ask ourselves what

happens to the souls of these women years from now after their conscience has matured, and they have had time to fully process their physical involvement in the intentional killing of their child. Whereas before, they were in a sterile environment, made to feel comfortable, soft music playing in the background, constantly being reassured by an assistant they were doing the right thing. They felt very little and saw even less. Now that they've become abortionists, they must manage days of heavy bleeding, cramps, fever, nausea, and, worst of all, the disposal of their dead baby, which the imagery will never be erased.

No doubt, many are so relieved they're no longer pregnant that they may not feel a pang of guilt. But as we know relief often gives way to regret, and regret to remorse when it all comes rushing back. With so many post-abortive women suffering from post-traumatic stress disorders (PTSD) after having a doctor-assisted abortion, is it unreasonable to suspect that many of these do-it-yourself abortionists are an emotional ticking time bomb? It stands to reason that we're on our way to seeing an explosion of post-abortive women suffering from PTSD far exceeding the women who had an abortion before the DIY days. The *Blueprint* offers pastors the strategy that helps women bypass the emotional fallout from the high risk of these do-it-yourself abortions. In the next chapter I talk about one solution that women are being deliberately denied information on.

Abortion Pill Reversal

It is widely accepted that the ability to reconsider one's decisions is part of the everyday human experience. So, it's appalling to see that as it relates to a woman's right to have a change of heart after taking the first drug, mifepristone, that doesn't apply. All women are aware of the abortion pill used for medical abortions; almost none are aware that it can be reversed if taken in time, and the abortion rights lobby intends to keep it that way.

Life coaches—referring to those who work at Heartbeat International's 24-hour hotline—have reported that women and men are so relieved and overjoyed when they find out they don't have to follow through with their fateful choice, they break down sobbing like a death row inmate just minutes away from being executed hearing that they've received a pardon. The abortion pill protocol recommendation is within 24 hours after taking the first abortion drug, mifepristone. The medical provider prescribes bioidentical progesterone to outnumber and outcompete the mifepristone to reverse the effects. An ultrasound is performed as soon as possible to confirm the pregnancy's heart rate, placement, and dating. Medical professionals use progesterone treatment to try and reverse the effects of mifepristone during the first trimester of pregnancy. This treatment, which uses the natural hormone progesterone, is effective in saving 64-68% of pregnancies that would have otherwise been terminated through the use of an abortion pill. Interestingly, despite claiming to aim for fewer abortions, Planned Parenthood has begun researching the creation of a combined pill containing both drugs, which would make it impossible to reverse the effects of mifepristone. It seems odd that this would come from a group proclaiming they're all about freedom of choice. That appears true as long as that choice is to abort.

CHAPTER 8

How Men Really Feel About Abortion

Since a man can't make one, he doesn't have a right to tell a woman when and where to create one. -T. Shakur

Lyrics like this from the late Rapper Tupac Shakur make it easy to see why abortion advocates believe men should sit down and shut up.

Mr. Shakur was like many who fail to realize that women do not give life, they give birth. A child receives an equal amount of DNA from both parents during conception, which involves both a man and a woman equally. However, more fundamentally, life comes from God. No humans can control it, whether men or women. Women do not make or control life, so they do not have the choice to end it.

Many men struggle in silence, trying to cope with the loss of their children through abortion, even though they may have participated in the decision to abort and assisted their partners in doing so. Though not nearly as much research has been done on abortion's effects on men as on women, considerable evidence shows that abortion often negatively affects men's mental health and that a large proportion of men regret their partner's abortion weeks or even years after.

There is a prevalent issue where men remain quiet about the emotional pain caused by abortions. Society has deemed abortion as a "woman's issue," and therefore, men should not have an opinion on it. This leaves the father feeling helpless and isolated, regardless of whether he agreed with the decision to have an abortion initially.

An article was recently published on the NBC Today Show website, which shared a positive experience of their partner's abortion. It was a predictable move for the Pro-Choice network. However, Care Net conducted their own study to examine how men feel about abortion. NBC wants us to believe that all men are Pro-Choice, but Care Net's research painted a much more intricate picture, contrary to what the abortion rights activists want us to believe.

A national survey was conducted on 1,000 men who had participated in an abortion. The survey asked them the same questions that a group of women had been asked a few years earlier about their experiences with abortion. The survey found that even among the population that had participated in an abortion, the majority did not advocate for the mother of their child to abort their baby. Four in ten recommended their partner have an abortion. Six in ten either said nothing or advocated for life. It's amazing how NBC was not able to find any of those guys for their story. A deeper look at this data does suggest some troubling news when you divide the men into three groups:

• Advocating for abortion.

• Advocating for life.

• Advocating for neither.

But first the bad news. Fully half of the men in the survey were attending church at least once per month at the time of the first abortion.

Unfortunately, one-third of the men who were surveyed belonged to the group that remained silent, not advocating either for or against. These men seemed to agree with the statement "no womb no say." While this is disappointing, it does hint at a silver lining.

It is reasonable to assume that most fathers who remain silent about the decision of whether to keep or abort a baby prefer the woman to keep the baby. This is because if a man does not want to be a father, it is too risky for him to stay quiet. He would likely express his desire for the woman to have an abortion because it would be costly for him to provide financial support for a child he does not want. It is important to note that even if the father chooses not to be involved in raising the child, he is still required to provide financial support through child support and other means. Therefore, it is likely that the one in three men who remain silent could be encouraged to become advocates for choosing life, in addition to the one in four men who already do so.

This is particularly true, because as earlier reported that the father is the most influential person in their decision to undergo an abortion. Men reported the same. However, the question that remains is whether his influence will be in favor of life or abortion.

In addition, the survey highlights the immense opportunity for the church to play a positive role in advocating for life. Fully half of the men in the survey were attending church at least once per month at the time of the first abortion they participated in. Notice at the time of their "first" abortion, indicating multiple abortions in their background. Four in ten of the women surveyed were regularly attending church.

This confirms abortion is a problem in the church—not just outside of it. However, men in the survey had positive attitudes about how the church could help couples with their pregnancy decisions. Just over half of the men believed churches are a safe place to talk about pregnancy options. Half of them also agreed pastors are sensitive to the pressures a man faces with an unplanned pregnancy.

According to a recent survey, three out of every five people believe that the church is ready to assist couples who want to keep their babies even if the pregnancy was unplanned, regardless of whether this belief is accurate or not. Therefore, the church should feel both disappointed and encouraged by this data. Although abortions are occurring at an alarming rate among Christians, the church can take heart in the fact that whether wishful thinking or not, most believe that it is prepared to offer support to those who need it.

It seems that even though some people who attend church may support the idea of abortion, they still believe that churches have a responsibility to help people make choices that lead to giving birth. Now that Roe is no more, we can use this information in a few ways. For one, we should take note in the fact that it's important to involve men in discussions about women's rights and decision-making. They are the most influential factor in a woman's decision. However, our culture has convinced many of them to remain silent. Insisting that men have no voice is sexist. Let's debunk this flawed thinking and inspire men to use their voices to exercise their God-given right to speak up for the life of the preborn child.

CHAPTER 9

Do We Owe Women An Apology?

After Adam had a time of reflection, I've questioned was he ever led to apologize to Eve. Did he care enough about how her life was affected to apologize for his role in not protecting her? Most likely like most of us, he prized his role as leader— an element of the male ego. However, one of the responsibilities of a leader is to "fess up" after we realize we've messed up. At the top of our responsibility chart though is protecting those in our care. That includes protecting them from themselves when necessary. In Genesis we see the first lapse of masculine leadership when Adam allowed Eve to take the lead. The fact that it was she that first wanted the "forbidden" didn't hold water with God as an excuse. Apparently, he wanted "it" too, but didn't want his share of the consequences. Adam seemed uncertain or unwilling to "fess up" that it was his failure that allowed Eve to be caught in that predicament. God would step in make it clear to him and all who came after him where the failure lied, "Adam, where art thou?!"

Like Adam many of us have allowed and often put women in vulnerable predicaments where they ended up getting caught between the proverbial rock and a hard place. Then rather than man up and accept responsibility for the situation we helped create, we encouraged and even coerced them into actions that were contrary to their instinctual nature, singing lead vocals on the Pro-Choice movement's biggest hit, "It's your body, it's your choice." Lyrics that in a practical sense can lure a mother, especially a young mother into making a choice with lifelong consequences.

Abortion is a forced attempt to reverse a mother's instinctual nature from one that nurtures and protects life to one that terminates it without any regard for the inevitable psychological consequences.

I recall when growing up on the farm. The only time the momma cow would become aggressive with us was when we got ready to separate her from calf. Once we got the calf and took it away, that momma cow would walk the fence for days mooing where she last saw her calf. I didn't understand it like I do now, but what we had done was take a part of her she could never get back.

No woman *wants* an abortion. A woman *wants* an abortion like an animal caught in a trap wants to gnaw its' leg off to get free. Regrettably the cost of getting free that way lives with her forever. With that said, it seems to me we owe women an apology.

When examining the available data on abortions in the United States it's clear that the circumstances that led to a woman's unplanned pregnancy and subsequent abortion remain with her long after her baby dies. Abortion eliminated the baby but not the other factors that led to the risk of abortion such as poverty, physical abuse, drug abuse, sexual abuse, poor relationship skills, and on and on. A study on the psychological effects of abortion published in America's Medical *Association of General Psychiatry* found that a full 20% of women experience profound regret, bouts of depression, self-loathing, bondage to guilt and grief and unforgiveness. A few years back I was in a prayer meeting where a woman praying cried out, "Lord, please forgive me for my abortions." Several things came to mind about that. One, the burden had gotten so heavy she couldn't carry it any longer. The other, like the woman in Luke 8:44 with the issue of blood, she'd been suffering a long time and gotten to the point she didn't care who knew. I don't know if that was the first time she's asked for forgiveness. It seems like we owe women an apology.

Despite all the evidence of the negative emotional side-effects of abortion the Pro-Choice movement still demands that she bow to their unwritten rule that you never speak negatively about your abortion experience. Nor is the media to report on it. So, she paints a smile on her face and lives with it, pretending all is well. Just "grin and bear," take one for the team. Throw in our insensitivity to how abortion can attack the soul of a woman in part because of the painted smile, and we're blinded to the psychological harm in many cases we helped create. In all fairness though there are some who are sensitive to her plight but due to the extremely sensitive nature of abortion are unsure how to address it. Yet still, it seems we owe women an apology.

Once her abortion is complete, there's no counseling, no assistance offered. No support from her church. It's all on her now. The abortion provider's focus was on abortion simply as a financial transaction, and not as a life transformational that so many women seeking abortion desperately needed. Half return for a second go round. Based on how God dealt with his man, Adam we owe women an apology. Perhaps we could see it clearer if we look at them as not just women, but our women—our daughters, our mother's, our grandmother's, our sisters, our aunts. An apology is a good starting place, but we owe them more. We owe them pregnancy care ministries for the abortion vulnerable such as *Making Life Disciples*, and pregnancy after-care ministries such as *Forgiven and Set Free* for struggling post- abortive women (and men) so the healing process can begin. I believe if we'll pause for a minute, we'll hear God calling out again. This time, "Men of God where art thou?"

CHAPTER 10

Pro-Life or Really Pro-Infant?

The consistent rap against Pro-Life, as unfair as it has been, is that we're more pro-infant than we are Pro-Life—that we only care about the child while it's inside of the womb. This charge is primarily led by my community, despite the fact from its inception, beginning with the Negro Project, this racially targeted movement had black unborn babies in its crosshairs for restricting our pro-liferation. So, a movement that is more of a ministry than a movement often finds itself constantly on the defense, trying to prove that our concern extends beyond the womb carrying the preborn child.

We can recite a laundry list of verifiable acts of kindness towards women and their babies after they've given birth; rental assistance, bus tokens for post-natal visits, diapers, clothes for her, clothes for her baby, strollers, car seats, and baby cribs. We even provide fatherhood training for the new dad. We are the largest group of donors by far and the biggest group of volunteers to maternity homes. Millions of Pro-Life individuals back up their Pro-Life worldview by providing homes for the millions of unwanted in foster care. We're the largest single group that provides permanent homes by way of adoption. Still, it's not enough.

The Pro-Choice community counters that even though you adopted and fostered hundreds of thousands of kids, that's just a drop in the bucket for what's needed. And although you've donated hundreds of millions of dollars in services that too is only a drop in the bucket for what's needed. No matter what we do, we can't seem to convince them that our support extends beyond the infant in the womb.

The largest percentage of these charitable acts are directed towards women and kids from my community—the very group that's leading the charge and claiming that it's not enough.

To the discerning mind, one might assess that it's all just a smokescreen to avoid thinking about what abortion does to a living, breathing defenseless human being while in the womb.

I am at a loss as to why saving a life is not considered a good and righteous act on its own, regardless of whether we commit to the long-term care of the life we saved. Essentially, some people argue that if we don't commit to the long-term care of babies after they're born, then saving their lives is not a good and righteous act because it didn't go far enough. This means that the good Samaritan in Luke 10 was not actually good because he didn't agree to care for the man on the side of the road for the rest of his life.

Picture watching the evening news and seeing a group of people gathered outside a house that had caught fire. They were unhappy and complaining because a firefighter had just entered the burning house and rescued a baby who was trapped inside. The people were upset because they had asked the firefighter if he would take care of the baby after rescuing her, but he had said no. They believed that it was unfair for him to leave the responsibility of caring for the baby to others. What aggravated them the most was that they had informed the firefighters that the baby's parents and grandparents had already passed away in the fire, and he saved the baby's life anyway.

This scenario reveals that the value of a good deed is not based on any pledges made after the deed is done. Saving a child's life is an inherently good act, regardless of any promises made afterward. We don't require firefighters, paramedics, or heart surgeons to make promises to care for the people they save. However, the abortion rights movement has convinced millions of people to believe in a twisted narrative that suggests the act of saving a life is only valuable if certain conditions are met and in and of itself does not hold intrinsic value.

The definition of being Pro-Life means that our priority is to protect life. Just as it doesn't diminish the good deed of the firefighter or anyone else who saves a life, accusations that we're not doing enough doesn't diminish the great work that Pro-Life people do and have done for nearly fifty years. If it were not for the Pro-Life movement, instead of 60 million tiny humans put down, that number may very well be 200 million.

According to the train of thought, saving a life is not enough unless you have a plan to support the life afterward. It is possible, then, for someone to excuse themselves and live their entire life without offering a helping hand to anyone because they rationalize, they are unable to provide long-term support.

When Pro-Choice people make "all we care about" accusations, what they're really saying is if a baby survives the womb, then we will help. But we're not going to lift a finger to ensure the child lives. I know this is a true statement because they allocate all of their energy and resources to removing obstacles to abortion, but they do not allocate any resources to removing obstacles for women who want to give birth.

To take their accusation one step further that the Pro-Life community doesn't do enough for children after they're born. To that, I say to the Pro-Choice community, you have the same obligation as we do. It's not just Pro-Life people that have this obligation. Pro-Choice people do too. But meet it in a way that does not create additional problems for those facing unplanned pregnancies while addressing the root causes.

CHAPTER 11

Gun Violence: A Reminder God Will Not Be Mocked?

- Six Killed, 12 Injured when gunman opens fire on crowd as they left night club.

- White gunman kills 10 black shoppers in Buffalo New York at Supermarket.

- Uvalde Texas teenage gunman massacres 19 children and two teachers.

- Three killed, several others wounded when gunman drove around looking for people to kill streaming it on Facebook Live.

- Three members of the University of Virginia football team shot dead in parking garage.

- Chesapeake Virginia Walmart supervisor kills six co-workers then kills himself.

- Boy, 11, innocent bystander fatally shot in Dallas by teen girl shooting at another girl.

> Headlines like these appear daily on our local and national news channels, social media feeds, and our newspapers. These are just a small example of the mass shootings that have become a plague and are getting worse. Still, they don't include what I described as knucklehead violence:

- Detroit man shot to death after he failed to hold open an elevator door.

- In Tulsa man shot his stepfather after argument over a monopoly game.

- Atlanta Subway employee shot and killed for putting too much mayonnaise on a sandwich.

- In Brooklyn MacDonalds employee shot in the neck cause: French fries cold.

- Houston man confessing to killing first person he saw in area where brother bought drugs.

When you add in road rage killings, domestic disputes, and petty arguments, it's clear that life doesn't hold very much value. Some say it's too many guns and we need more gun control. Others say we need a ban on assault weapons. Others, background checks and longer waiting periods. Others, more police protection. What is missing in this discourse is the declining value our culture places on human life. When a society no longer places value and emphasis on the importance of life itself, what transpires is what we see daily in the headlines. Abortion and other anti-life legislation have contributed to the disregard for life. From the continued advocacy for no restrictions on abortion to states that have passed assisted suicide legislation, the value on human life, "endowed by our creator," has eroded like sand on a seashore.

I mentioned earlier about Montana passing a Born Alive Act allowing a baby that survived an abortion to suffer a slow death at the mother's request. As believers, don't we have to think about consequences of the message it sends to our youth on the importance of human life?

Abortion is a vicious backhand in the face of the Creator of life that has left us with some "hellish" reminders that God will not be mocked. We understand it's as immutable as the law of gravity. We may even get by for a while, but we can never escape. Galatians 6:7 describes it as the law of sowing and reaping. In Paul's writing to the church in Galatia he starts off with a warning, "Do not be deceived" (Galatians 6:7 NKJV). In other words, don't fool yourself. Don't think that it doesn't come back to you. The verse continues with "God is not mocked." Don't think you're going to make a fool out God and invalidate his word. It continues on, "whatever a man sows" we reap in kind. " . . . that shall he also reap." In the words of the late Dr. Charles Stanley, "We reap it later and we reap it greater."

Am I off base when I suggest that our out-of-control violence is the spiritual principle of sowing and reaping in effect? *Whatsoever* you sow—sow love, reap love. Sow hate, reap hate. Sow life, reap life. Sow death, reap death?

In Second Kings we see the law of sowing and reaping

in effect as well. God's chosen people had begun engaging in the heathen practice of child sacrifice to appease the pagan God of Molech (Jer.32–35). These now Pro-Choice "Christians" had been seduced into, *my child my choice.* They believed they had the right to toss their newborns onto the white-hot outstretched arms of a pagan idol and somehow, they'd receive a blessing. Infanticide and abortion both are sacrificial acts made for the benefit of an expected return. Yet, they still brought their tithes to the Temple, but their most valuable possessions they brought to Molech. They couldn't connect the dot of cause-and-effect. In either case, they found out that by devaluing their infants' lives they devalued their own. Homicides and assaults skyrocketed so greatly that God had Joshua (Joshua 20) establish cities of refuge where the accused could escape to avoid becoming a victim of mob justice.

These sickening headlines represent a clear devaluation of human life. It's irrefutable evidence that if preborn life doesn't matter then life doesn't matter. As a society, once we determine we're not going to value the life that's inside the womb, whether we acknowledge it or refuse to accept it, the spiritual ramifications are we've just determined the value of life outside the womb also. Expecting a different outcome is as ridiculous as a farmer planting corn while expecting melons. It's an inviolable law, and it can't be suspended to satisfy our preferred outcome. We've made our bed, now we must lie in it.

So, the issue on the table before us is our valuation of life—not unborn life, but life itself. We cannot make a distinction. Poor life, rich life, black life, white life, brown life, disabled life, elderly life, unborn life—is it to be respected and protected? When we take the protection off one the eventual result is we've taken the protection off all.

The uncomfortable truth is that for nearly fifty years, we've nurtured a culture of violence and death by embracing the various deceptions empowered by the forces of darkness that control the pro-abortion movement. In doing so, we've sown the unborn-life-doesn't-matter-seed and are now reaping a frightening harvest that life doesn't matter. That's transforming our public spaces into mindless shooting galleries.

And even though we've finally put an end to the government-sponsored slaughter of millions of unborn lives, our kids, grandkids, and even great-grandchildren will still be chewing on the bitter fruit of this seed long after we've gone. It's too late to pray for crop failure. The seed is already in the ground. However, I am excited that just a few pages away is a righteous seed. If sown from the pulpit it will begin to produce a harvest that many will enjoy for a thousand generations.

CHAPTER 12

Systemic Racism and Its Influence on Black Abortion Rates

This topic has been challenging. As a black man, systemic racism has undeniably had an influence on every aspect of my life and all blacks to some degree. The impact of this so-called abortion rights movement has left a trail of tears and blood in my community that stretches from one end of the Mississippi to the other. So great is the problem it must be exposed for what it is. An injustice that began by one racial group and continued by another.

No one would ever suspect a character like Hip-Hop mogul Diddy, formerly known as Sean P. Diddy Combs, is Pro-Life. In the remake of the 1940s classic *A Raisin in the Sun*, starring Sidney Poitier, he plays the legendary actor. Although it was appropriate, it certainly was unnecessary for him to influence the writers to insert a line in the script.

The setting is inner-city Chicago, where a poor black extended family lives together in a cramped second-floor tenement flat. One minute, Combs jumps for joy, flying high, when his wife reveals that she's expecting. Suddenly, the mood shifts when his mother drops a bombshell: his wife has secretly visited a woman in the "hood" known for abortions. Financial struggles were an everyday experience, as it was for virtually all black families in the 40s. Nonetheless, he was a proud, hardworking God-fearing black man. At that moment, he had heard more than his mind could absorb and exploded into an uncontrollable rage. He grabbed his coat and bolted through the door, slamming it hard behind him. Hours later, when sobriety had replaced rage, he slowly walked in and quietly plopped down at the small breakfast table.

In a solemn voice barely a few decibels above a whisper, he makes a poignant announcement to his wife and everyone with a listening ear, including the movie viewers, "Ruth, we are a people that give life, not take it away." That's one way of letting the world know where you stand on the life issue.

Throughout our history, from the Ivory Coast of Africa to the Antebellum plantations of the South, our people have always celebrated new life. Even while enduring the harsh realities of slavery, and the decades of the repressive Jim Crow laws, we viewed new life as a precious gift. The passing of Roe in 1973 was a significant moment for the country, but for my community, it represented the beginning of an even greater decline. It prompted the Reverend Jesse Jackson to courageously make a prophetic pronouncement that codifying Roe into law would become a form of black genocide. Unfortunately, his prophecy has been fulfilled.

So how did we go from celebrating new life to creating these illogically high abortion rates among black women, where they terminate life five times more than white women? I want to stop here and preface the remainder of this chapter with a much-needed clarification. I am not someone who sees a racist behind every tree. But the irrefutable truth is that this great country of ours was founded on a racist ecosystem where discriminatory policies were embedded in every nook and cranny of society to hinder the advancement and achievements of black people from the cradle to the grave to maintain a feeling of white supremacy.

Nine generations removed from chattel slavery we're still being stung by the deleterious effects of a racist ecosystem that continues to bleed through the centuries. Manifesting disparities into virtually every sphere of black life from our education system to our justice system to our healthcare system to employment to economic inclusion and so-called abortion "rights."

Abortion "rights" as they're called have produced sordid outcomes where the lives of black babies are terminated in staggering numbers compared to all other groups. Surprisingly, those who should be crying foul continue to push forth the subtle narrative; it's in our best interest. If there were a system in place where, decade after decade, the rules of the game always had the hometown finishing in last place, would not the leaders of the team cry—foul?

Even when laws and regulations may be equally applied, yet produce unequaled racial outcomes, we understand that it's still racist regardless of intent. Simply from a humanitarian viewpoint, when black babies are being put to death at a rate five times greater than that of white babies while making up a fraction of the population, and black women face the emotional fallout in far greater numbers than all other groups, someone needs to call that a foul.

Well, I'm calling it. Foul, foul, foul!

On one hand, I find it hard to accept that all other forms of systemic racism with such flagrant inequities are attacked from all sides except this one. The only one that leads to a disproportionate number of poor black women being exploited and black babies being discarded like rotten meat. This stands alone at the apex of all other forms of systemic racism.

On the other hand, the psychological underpinnings of this anomaly of mass ambivalence can be partially explained with insights from the mind of the outspoken promoter of African American history and father of Black History Month, Carter G. Woodson. In his book, *The Miseducation of the Negro*, Mr. Woodson writes, "When you control a man's thinking you do not have to worry about his actions. You do not have to tell him to stand here or go yonder. He will find his proper place and will stay in it."

So, the stage was set. In a society that is built on racial unfairness, the laws, policies, and initiatives that are made by the powerful create imbalances that harm the already marginalized more than others. The Negro Project, the name alone suggests nefarious intent, fell into that category. Its success relied on a toxic blend of white superiority and black inferiority.

The brainchild of white feminist Margaret Sanger, founder of the Birth Control League and forerunner to 'Planned' Parenthood. The Negro Project planted the subliminal message in the hearts and minds of black people that some black lives; the poor, the poorly educated, the down and under, shouldn't matter. She saw this group as many obviously see them today: a lost cause and in the best interest of all, including them, if they were never born.

Being a staunch proponent of Adolf Hitler's eugenics movement, which in essence is the science of picking winners and losers, she saw it as a necessary evil to "weed out" those whom she deemed "the unfit, the dependent, delinquent, and defective elements in modern society." Where Hitler chose militarism to carry out his immoral ideology against the Jews, Sanger relied on distorted logic riding a wave of deception while cloaked in compassion.

Hitler's legacy against the Jewish race, as awful as it was, will forever pale in comparison to Sanger's legacy and the injurious effect it has had and is having on my community.

It was sold under the pretense of better health and family planning. Better health? Normally we expect health programs to focus on life-threatening health issues like strokes, high blood pressure, heart attacks, diabetes, etc. It certainly encompasses far more than unfettered access to free birth control. Nor is it listed in any medical journal as some would have you believe—taking the life of a normal healthy baby considered healthcare. Ms. Sanger's subsequent writings confirm that "better health" was not her aim for the black community.

Her family "planning" was closer to resembling family eradication. Sanger cleverly implemented her Negro Project by enlisting the help of community powerbrokers and pastors. She wrote, "The minister's work is also important. We do not want word to go out that we want to exterminate the Negro population. The minister is the only man who can straighten out that idea if it ever occurs to any of their more rebellious members."

Sanger's goal was not to get rid of all blacks. It was only a certain type of black that found itself in her crosshairs. The poor and supposedly 'less intelligent' that she described as racially inferior "disposal stock" are the ones that she felt should be sterilized and segregated onto farms to prevent procreation. It was sold just as some political leaders are selling it today, under the guise of giving women control over their bodies when, in truth, it was as it is now meant to be a method to address poverty and high birth rates.

If Sanger were alive today, she'd go after those who live in the margins of life. At the top of her hit list would be poor young single black females followed by recipients of Aid to Families with Dependent Children (AFDC). All those below the poverty line would be at risk. The organization that replaced the one she founded, Planned Parenthood, is continuing her legacy. By her writings even the children in St. Jude's hospital would likely be somewhere on her radar.

To the discerning mind, if she was so concerned about the well-being of the Negro, it seems like she should have included in her meeting with the "minister man" discussions on anti-poverty programs like quality education, voting rights, ending Jim Crow, and anti-lynching laws. It seems like her "compassion" for the poor Negro would have led her to pick at least one from a long list of inequities to propose to the "minister man". That could have helped Negroes rise above the racist ecosystem that she helped maintain, to keep the white man's boot firmly on the necks of blacks, while her race gained a 300-year head start to upward mobility.

After all, if she cared so much about the Negro, most would consider it her reasonable act of service. Especially when you consider it had been only a little over a generation since we had been freed from three centuries of being used as subhuman beasts of burden and treated as even less. At a minimum, her "compassionate" heart should have led her to disavow the terrorist acts being carried out against us by the Klu Klux Klan. Instead she validated that immoral and reprehensible organization of snivelling hooded cowards by becoming one of their most requested speakers.

My cynical mind says she met with them for a congratulatory pat on the back after she announced they could put away their gas cans and torches since she had just cleverly sold us a concept that would do the work for them.

Systemic racism's influence behind these tragically, shamefully, and needlessly high abortion rates that survive on the exploitation of poor black females cannot be denied or underestimated. Fifty years ago, Reverend Jackson was the first to sound the alarm, alerting us to the significant harm that would be done to black people. Mr. Woodson continued to sound the alarm on the effects of systemic injustice until the day he died. His synopsis points a straight arrow at how and why we've allowed ourselves to be exploited, and abortion rights misidentified as being in our best interest and added to the list of sacred cows. I can hear the late straight-talking, straight-shooting Malcolm X proclaiming, "We've been misled, had . . . took!" The good news is after a half-century of having the dubious distinction decade after decade of taking home the blue ribbon for the number of black babies aborted, and the number of black women left emotionally scarred, more of us on the hometown team are now "woke" and crying foul! We're awakening to the fact that regardless of previous conditioning unborn black lives matter, too!

CHAPTER 13

The Life-Saving Role Of Pregnancy Resource Centers

Once known as Crisis Pregnancy Centers, several years ago, they agreed to be called pregnancy resource centers. Some clients were offended by being declared they were in crisis. But since the beginning, these centers have always drawn the Pro-Choice supporters and the media's ire for offering women an alternative to abortion.

There have been instances where certain groups have spread false and misleading information to harm the reputation of crisis pregnancy centers. Unfortunately, many churches refuse to provide financial or prayer support to these centers. Following the overturning of Roe, many centers were subjected to hateful phone calls, break-ins, vandalism, arson, and physical attacks on workers. In July 2022, Sen. Elizabeth Warren of Massachusetts expressed her desire to shut down all crisis pregnancy centers in her state.

The truth is Pregnancy Resource Centers (PRCs) should be renamed life support centers. Because every day, they are providing a lifeline for the babies whose mothers would have no other choice but to abort. They are Christian-based nonprofit organizations devoted to offering women alternatives to abortion, helping them make informed choices, and providing a range of services to support them throughout their pregnancy and beyond.

Many services are available in low-income and at-risk

areas to offer families the crucial resources and support they need during difficult times. These services are mainly provided by Christian women, who are mostly white but serve predominantly black and brown communities. They are compassionate about the mothers and their unborn babies, and they operate with faith, not knowing how they will fulfill all the demands or where they will get the necessary support. They understand women don't wake up wanting an abortion. There's something driving her to think she has no other choice. Whatever that something is, it generally boils down to — fear—and that fear is often magnified by the feeling that she's all alone in her pregnancy.

She may be abortion-minded because she thinks there's no one to help her. In addition, there may be other people who are upset, disappointed, or angry with — her—or would be if they even knew she was pregnant. She may even feel disappointed or angry with herself. PRCs skillfully work to find out what fear is driving her to think that abortion is the only option.

When a woman faces an unplanned pregnancy, it can be a difficult and isolating experience. Unlike when we experience an injury or illness, and people rally around us, many women in this situation feel completely alone. Many times, they walk in overwhelmed with embarrassment and regret, compounded oftentimes by being abandoned by their partner. The compassionate women operating Pregnancy Resource Centers have wholeheartedly committed themselves to assisting women and couples facing challenging circumstances; women walk in feeling hopeless and leave feeling relieved. They're grateful for the emotional support they desperately needed as well as the material support and valuable resources to help navigate the difficult journey ahead.

PRCs offer a variety of support services to help individuals overcome any obstacles they may face when choosing to give birth to their child. One of the most important needs is material support. The center has a room they call the Material Support Room. It's filled with donated items that mothers can select from, including car seats, baby diapers, wipes, cribs, strollers, baby clothes, and even maternity clothes for expectant mothers. In addition to material assistance, PRCs also provide birthing and parenting classes, relationship training, fatherhood mentoring, and sometimes gas cards and rental assistance.

In most cases, organizations that assist expectant mothers have a client advocate who meets with them to understand their situation and why they are considering different options for their pregnancy. This advocate may also share the Gospel message with those open to it. These mothers are often stressed and may appreciate having someone to pray with and discuss God's love. If they require services that the organization does not directly provide, they typically work with other agencies to ensure the mother receives the necessary support.

They specialize in networking, gathering information, and developing relationships with various community organizations. Every center is a one-stop location for pregnancy-help resources; most have a long list of partners to provide services as needed. Such as:

- Women and Infant Children (WIC) to get food into a pregnant woman's home.

- Working with health services agencies to ensure she has everything she needs for ongoing care.

- Contacting government agencies to ensure she's signed up for any help she qualifies.

- Working with hospitals to provide labor and birthing classes on-site at the center.

PRCs have many needs themselves.

Financial support is always at the top of the wish list for Pregnancy Resource Centers. Many founders/operators work without a salary and often dip into their pockets to pay rent or buy diapers or formula for last-minute emergencies. PRCs have a strong relationship with the faith community, as that is typically the only way they can offer so many services for free or at a minimal cost. Thus, financial support from churches is crucial for the survival of PRCs.

Some rely on churches for rent-free space to operate. Others request their members to donate slightly used items for their material room. Some hold diaper drives, because diapers are always in short supply. I've heard reports of babies being cranky for no apparent reason until an irritating diaper rash that resulted from not being able to change diapers as needed was discovered.

PRCs, unlike abortion providers such as Planned Parenthood, do not receive any federal funds. They rely solely on donations from individuals and organizations. Monthly contributions of $25, $50, or $100 help them keep their operations going. Additionally, they often hold annual fundraising banquets to help sustain them throughout the year.

Volunteers are always welcome and needed. Support

doesn't always have to come in the form of money. Without volunteers, they wouldn't be able to provide the variety of services their clients require for free. Volunteers serve various roles, such as receptionists, patient advocates, call center operators, material support room organizers, and counselors.

Volunteers may be used to coordinate and host baby showers and serve as volunteer mentors for young women who need a caring role model. PRCs can use volunteers to pray for the women who come in or someone to teach a relationship or parenting class. Volunteers may even be needed to do simple tasks like sweeping the floor. Men must also counsel and mentor young fathers, as engaging with the father is crucial. The father is the one person who can turn a crisis into a celebration. Men who weren't planning on being involved in the child's life changed their minds simply because a male mentor spoke plainly to them. An older man shared his thoughts during a discussion about the joys and responsibilities of being a dad. This discussion inspired many young men to rise and become involved in their children's lives. Some even went on to marry their child's mother and build a good life together.

For those who have recognized their need for Christ, there is a place to grow in their faith and a group to grow with. This group includes other moms, but more importantly, the church.

Most PRCs offer post-abortive support for women who've undergone an abortion and are suffering emotionally. This help can be private counseling, classes, or small support groups. Loving and supporting women who choose abortion is the ultimate goal. PRCs offer a secure environment for women to share their experiences and emotions while also assisting them in finding physical, emotional, and spiritual healing. This role refutes one common accusation against pregnancy resource centers and Pro-Lifers in general—that our only concern is that the baby is born, with little thought given to helping the mothers and children afterward.

Senators like Miss Warren have gone on the warpath against pregnancy resource centers that doing the Lord's work is severely misguided. Providing compassion, hope, and help for those facing difficult pregnancy decisions is a labor of love for the women who run them. It's unimaginable what the death toll would be without their presence. Rather than 60 million, it could have easily reached 200 hundred million or more. PRCs deserve our praise and all the support we can give them. When you fully understand the difference they make every day in the lives of people in the most desperate situations, it forces you to say, "Thank you, God, for sending these angels of hope." As you will discover in the chapter detailing the blueprint, they play a crucial role in making abortion an unnecessary option in the church.

CHAPTER 14

SOS: Call of Desperation to the Church

It's here! The overturning of Roe has created the predicted tidal wave of expectant mothers and fathers who once saw abortion as the silver bullet to unplanned pregnancies. The church is the only way we can address the needs of an estimated 450,000 to 600,000 women who need our help now that Roe is no more.

The long-awaited end to this homegrown Holocaust that has sent millions of defenseless babies to a watery grave is undoubtedly worthy of a huge celebration. But help is needed now more than ever before.

The president of Care Net saw this coming when he looked at another watershed moment in our nation's history—the abolitionist movement. The abolitionists successfully advocated for the end of slavery but overlooked the necessity of the care component once slavery was over. Consequently, the end of slavery was followed by decades of Jim Crow, where black people walked off the plantation as slaves and back on as sharecroppers.

The three main pillars of society—government, business, and faith—failed to anticipate and develop a strategy to integrate black people into the fabric of mainstream society. As he looked around, he could see the same level of unpreparedness in these same pillars of society. They, and we, failed to address the need for compassionate solutions for women and men facing difficult pregnancy decisions that are now left out in the "cold."

The year before Roe was overturned, there were a little over 600,000 abortions nationwide. Now consider this: there are only about 3,000 pregnancy care centers nationwide. It's mathematically impossible for 3,000 pregnancy care centers to absorb the massive increase in services. We saw that when Texas passed its fetal heartbeat bill, statewide pregnancy centers were overrun with women who were no longer able to obtain abortions and were now needing an alternative. The Texas state legislature succeeded in its advocacy for life but like the abolitionists, fell short in advocating the need for care—the solution: The local church.

There are approximately 400,000 churches in the U.S. If only 1% of them, a tiny percentage, created programs to reach abortion-vulnerable women in their church, that would mean an additional 4,000 points of compassion. If we could get 2%, that would mean an additional 8,000 points of compassion, bringing the total to 11,000 points of compassion.

Some may argue that this is the role of pregnancy centers; but James' order to see after the widows and orphans was to the church, not the pregnancy centers. Besides, there are not enough pregnancy care centers, and there can never be enough. Second, this is really a discipleship issue. The church is called to make disciples. Pregnancy centers can't make disciples. They can and do evangelize, but they can't make disciples. Discipleship requires an ongoing relationship. Third, not only is the church called to make disciples, but every "good work" that the church does—such as providing food for the hungry, homes for the homeless, and care for the pregnant—should be so they can come into a relationship with Jesus Christ.

For more information on Making Life Disciples
www.carenet.org/making life disciples

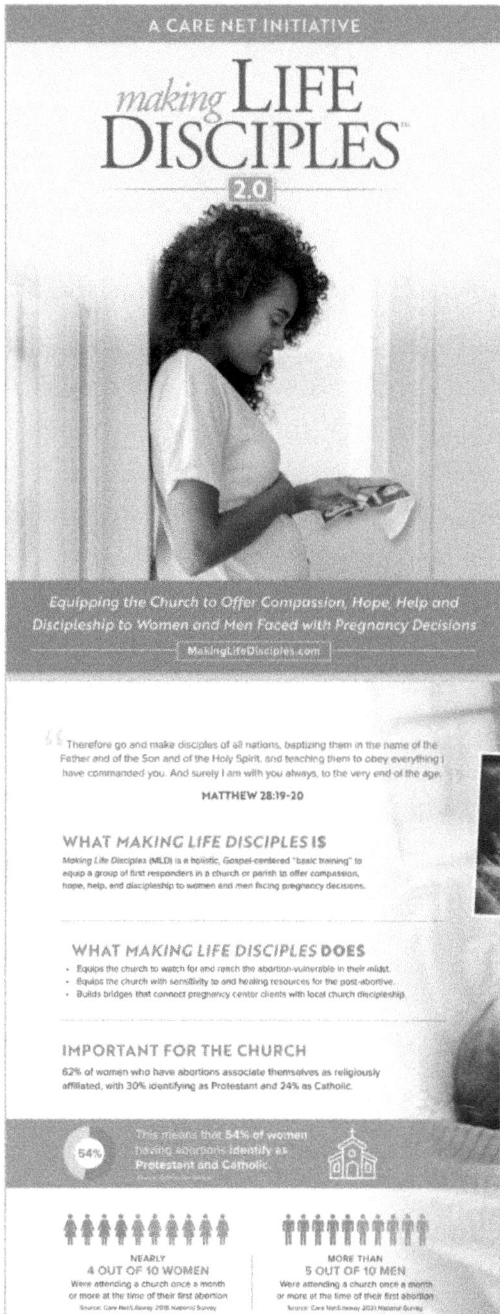

Everyone Jesus encountered received not only physical help but also spiritual guidance. Whether they had marital problems, demons, or needed healing, he addressed their deeper spiritual needs after meeting their physical ones. In other words, people came as they were but didn't stay as they came. They left transformed. Serving women and men vulnerable to abortion should be as crucial to the church as feeding the homeless, providing addiction programs, or any other social outreach project.

"Pregnancy centers are para-church ministry. They are there to help the church fulfill its mission, not vice versa. Care Net, anticipated the need for churches to help meet the increased demand for care. They have created an easily accessible online curriculum called Making Life Disciples. It's designed specifically for churches to form pregnancy care ministries to help abortion-vulnerable women and men in their congregations choose life for their unborn babies and abundant life for their families. The next chapter shows how we can win this war, but it will require the church's involvement. Without the church's involvement, millions and millions of unborn lives will be needlessly lost. And millions and millions of women and men will be saddled with shame and regret.

CHAPTER 15

The Blueprint to Ending Abortion in the Church

The Critical Role of the Pastor

I intentionally spent the greater portion of this book exposing misinformation and illogical arguments designed to win Christians' hearts. Now that Roe has been overturned in the courts, our focus must shift to overturning it in the hearts and minds of Christians, and it all begins with the pastor. The pastor has a critical role in making abortion an unnecessary option in the church. You heard how some of the loudest backlash came from Christians. You've read how 76% of women did not believe that churches have a ministry prepared to help them when facing an unplanned pregnancy. These women likely knew that abortion was wrong and violated their Christian values, but their circumstances made them believe they had no other "choice." The good news is that most in the church are not Pro-Choice by conviction but rather by circumstance, and a large percentage are straddling the fence. They're neither Pro-Life nor Pro-Choice; the pastor's job is not as much of an uphill climb as some would think. Hopefully, you see the considerable need for discipleship training in this area by now.

I experienced how much a few years back when speaking on an HBCU campus firsthand. When I asked the question, "Do black lives matter?" Without hesitation, they roared back, "Yes! Of course!" But when I asked what about unborn black life, suddenly their tongues were tied. They weren't sure. Or responded, "It depends." Whether it was the 20-year-old sophomore, or the 50-year-old professor didn't matter. These were not Neo-Nazis or the Proud Boys I was speaking to. These were people who looked like me and were supposedly Christian. Yet, they were confused as to how to respond. On the one hand, they knew an unborn black life matters to God and should matter to them especially. On the other hand, they seem unsure if they're willing to take a stand in defiance of allegiance to their political party's platform. Polls show that blacks aren't the only race that has that response. Therein lies the problem. Only the pastor can help them see the bigger picture; this is not a political issue. The more significant issue is life and the importance of valuing it. If we don't value life in the womb, we will not value it outside of it. And if unborn life doesn't matter, then life outside of the womb can't matter. Not yours, theirs, or mine. It can never be overemphasized. It's that important.

Abortion is more than a social or political issue; it is a profound spiritual battle that touches the core of our faith. As Christians, we believe that every life is sacred, created in the image of God (Genesis 1:27), and known by Him even before birth (Jeremiah 1:5). The fight against abortion is a defense of these fundamental truths. It challenges us to uphold life's sanctity and protect the most vulnerable among us. Ephesians 6:12 reminds us that our struggle is not merely against flesh and blood but against spiritual forces of evil. By engaging in this spiritual battle, we affirm God's sovereignty over life and stand as witnesses to His love and compassion for all His creation.

In this discipleship training, I believe the place to begin is within our journey of faith. Helping them understand the spiritual forces at play is crucial for every believer. Recognizing these spiritual realities equips us to stand firm in our beliefs, discern God's will, and live out our calling with courage and conviction. By deepening our awareness of the spiritual forces that influence our lives, we can better navigate our challenges, strengthen our relationship with God, and fulfill our divine purpose.

We're able to see these forces of darkness at work when we look back at how they manipulated Pharoah into killing all the male babies in an attempt to control the Hebrew population. We see it again in the New Testament when King Herod, trying to kill the Messiah, ordered the killing of all the male babies under two years of age.

These forces of darkness seek to kill and destroy everything close to the heart of God. Nothing the forces of darkness hate more than the imago dei. Next to the attacks on the image of God is the next creation in line, the family. We see that in the second chapter of Genesis. Once God brought Eve to Adam to begin a family that would accomplish his will on earth as it was in Heaven, the very next verse, the devil appeared. Helping Believers understand the reason we must stand against abortion is because it's an attack against the sanctity of life and an attack on the sanctity of marriage and family as God designed. Only a few understand that, and most never will unless the pastor or his designated appointee teaches them.

The Critical Role Of Discipleship

If we wonder how Jesus would respond to the issue of unwed pregnancy, we can look at how he approached the cultural issues of his day. One striking aspect of his ministry was that it always went against the prevailing culture around him. During Jesus's time, if an unmarried woman was found to be pregnant, Roman law allowed for infanticide, while Jewish law didn't support infanticide. Their solution was a cultural abortion. That meant, "putting her away". Since they couldn't put the baby away, they put the mother and the baby away together. Both groups sought to quickly move on from the situation by getting rid of the baby.

If the religious leaders were to bring her to Jesus in one of their efforts to trap him, saying, "Our law says to put her away, what say you?" Jesus, always one to cut straight to the heart of a matter, would likely respond, "Where is the Father?" He knows the best solution for addressing unwed pregnancies is not infanticide or single motherhood but marriage or responsible fatherhood.

God's original plan has always remained the same: to have a father and mother united in marriage, loving Him, loving each other, and loving their child. While God's will can be carried out in single-parent homes, it's clear that this wasn't His preferred method, as demonstrated by the call to Joseph. Simply putting a pregnant woman "away" is a band-aid solution like giving a man suffering from prostate cancer extra strength Tylenol. It may provide momentary relief, but the underlying issue remains.

Supporting a woman's choice to end her pregnancy is not in line with the values of Christianity. Unlike the Romans, who had their own justifications, we have the word of God and the spirit of God, as well as the example of how God handled Mary's unplanned pregnancy. In addition to the command to love our neighbor as ourselves. Our neighbor, as defined in the story of the good Samaritan, is anyone we see in need. A preborn baby is a neighbor.

If we adopt the practice of the Romans, we become guilty of spiritual malpractice on those seeking our help. Even the secular-based Alcoholics Anonymous acknowledges the need for what they call a higher power—not just to help alcoholics get sober but to stay sober. Supporting a woman either directly or indirectly by proxy for access to an abortion doesn't decrease the chances of her needing another one, which should be our goal.

The initial step in effectively solving a problem is to define it correctly. In this case, all of society assumes the problem is an unplanned pregnancy. The alcoholic's problem is not alcohol. The drug addict's problem is not drugs. More accurately, their problem is sin, transgressing the law of God. We can pass laws that prohibit them from buying alcohol. We can incarcerate them. But the sin problem is still present. The reason the unmarried woman or man is confronted with an unexpected pregnancy is sin. We can kill every unborn baby she conceives, but until the sin is put to death, we will have to keep on killing.

Only Jesus can kill sin. He not only commanded us to love our neighbor, but he also commanded us to introduce them to him, the sin killer. This command to make disciples is what's needed. Until we introduce them to Jesus their real problem is addressed. The culture doesn't know that. They think her problem is an unexpected pregnancy and abortion is the only solution they have for addressing it.

Jesus's message was always to come as you are but not to stay as you came. In every encounter, whether it was with the woman who had multiple husbands, the rich man with too much pride, or the naked man living amongst the catacombs cutting himself, Jesus did not seek to take away his knife. He recognized a spiritual deficiency. When he fed the multitudes, he also addressed their spiritual hunger by feeding them the *Bread of Life.*

A woman facing an unplanned pregnancy doesn't need an abortion. She needs to come into a life-changing relationship with Jesus Christ. Her preborn child and the child's father need to come into the same life-changing relationship. They need to become a disciple of Jesus Christ; as his disciples, we're the only ones who can do that.

Critical Need for Pregnancy Resource Partnerships

The church and pregnancy resource centers are a marriage-ordained in Heaven. The church is the David we need in our fight to cut the head off this Goliath and end abortion in the church. Many churches do a great job supporting food pantries, housing for single mothers, WIC programs, etc. And a small, unfortunately, percentage goes as far as supporting pregnancy resource centers. I must point out that apart from resource centers, all their support is after birth. She's deciding whether to have the abortion based on the support she's identified from conception to birth. Her child's life is weighing in the balance to the degree she can make those support pieces fit into a nine-month and nine-second window. As Roland Warren, president of Care Net, a network of almost 1,200 pregnancy care centers, often says, "Life decisions need life support that the church is uniquely positioned and called to provide." He goes on to point out how the Church is the only institution that's ideologically aligned and structurally capable of addressing the needs of abortion-vulnerable women and men facing pregnancy decisions in a God-honoring way. Social service agencies are great and can serve large numbers, but their services are a retail consumer-focused business that's transactional. Once the service is rendered, the transaction is over. Their greater need is for transformation. Yet, social service agencies are not in the business of addressing their deeper spiritual needs, which is creating the crisis. The church is. So, they're structurally capable but not ideologically aligned.

Faith-based pregnancy centers do an incredible job of meeting a woman's material needs from the time of conception up until around the age of three. But if a 15-year-old girl shows up and unless she needs diapers and baby wipes, there's not much they have to offer. So, they're ideologically aligned but not structurally capable of providing long-term support. The church is. As people of faith, we recognize that her best chance to avoid falling into the "18,18,18" trap is for her to become a disciple of Jesus Christ. Otherwise, she may return in 18 months with another pregnancy and another guy. Or, in 18 years with a pregnant daughter, or someone else's daughter her 18-year-old son impregnated When she becomes a disciple, her kids are likely to become disciples, increasing the odds that the cycle of inter-generational abortion is broken. Even though at the resource center, she may have recognized her need for a transforming relationship with Christ, without the church, she likely will go back and continue to be disciplined by the culture from which she came, Ultimately she will probably end up once again at a pregnancy help center or worse an abortion clinic.

New disciples require ongoing support that only the

church can provide. When we look at Jesus's ministry, we see that every "good" work was done so that they might become disciples. He met their immediate needs, but then he addressed their deeper spiritual need: transformation. If an abortion-vulnerable woman came to Jesus, he would address her immediate need to remove the obstacle preventing her from choosing life, but it wouldn't end there.

Like Jesus, every "good" work we do should be so that they might become his disciples. Whether providing food for the hungry, housing for the homeless, clothes for the naked, or compassion for the pregnant, it all should lead to discipleship. God often uses a crisis to soften a hard heart where they're willing to submit to his yoke and begin learning a better way to live. When we view the abortion issue through the eyes of Jesus, we see clearly that it's an opportunity to create disciples, and the resource centers are an untapped mission field that's white-hot with the harvest.

For that to take place, life-saving partnerships must be created with those who are the first line of defense for women and men facing complex pregnancy decisions— pregnancy resource centers. Pregnancy resource centers need churches for their clients to establish a relationship for ongoing support. Spiritual conversions can and often do occur at resource centers, but they can't make disciples. The church can. They need the church's help in removing obstacles in the path of the abortion-minded woman that stand in her way of choosing life. The obstacles vary. She may be a college student and can't afford a place to stay. Perhaps there's a church member that has a spare bedroom. Maybe the guy is afraid of becoming a father. There's likely a guy in the church who would gladly mentor him. She or he doesn't have a job. Maybe a business owner in the church needs someone or knows someone who has a job opening. Perhaps she needs a mature Christian woman to lean on.

Churches Need the Resource Centers, Too

Not only does the resource center need churches, but churches also need the resource centers. A large study revealed that 40% of women (50% of men) at the time of their first abortion were attending church at least once a month. And 54% of all women who had an abortion identify as Christians. So, there's a significant and troubling issue with abortion in the body of Christ. This points to the urgent need for the church to establish pregnancy care ministries. We have divorce care, grief care, substance abuse care, etc. Statistics say we need pregnancy care to prevent the unnecessary loss of life for the preborn. The resource centers are perfectly positioned to come alongside the church as a para ministry to help meet the needs of abortion-vulnerable women and men in their congregation.

There's one more reason why the church needs pregnancy resource centers. One of the effects of the fifty-year legacy of Roe v. Wade is that it's cut a wide swath through the body of Christ. So vast that nearly one in every pew sits in silence, either with regret or shame or both from having an abortion or aiding and abetting one. My fifteen years of experience in this space reveals that many were deeply wounded. The benefit is they possess an intimate understanding of what it's like to walk in the shoes of those facing unplanned pregnancies. Many would love nothing more than to help a young woman or man in some way to make a better choice than perhaps they did. All they need is opportunity. So, the church's role in a post-Roe world is to go! Go ye therefore into pregnancy resource centers and make ye disciples. Jesus commanded it.

Critical Need for Pregnancy Care Ministries

To end abortion in the church, we must establish pregnancy care ministries that offer compassion, hope, and help for those facing unplanned pregnancy decisions. Or at least partner up with another church that does.

The pastor is the one who can explain how James (1:27) informs us of our obligation to see after widows and orphans. James wrote that a widow was a woman without a husband and an orphan was a child without a father, which meant that the husband and father were dead. Today, the proverbial husband and father are saying to the mother and child you're dead to me, creating cultural widows and orphans that we identify as single mothers and children. In biblical times, just as in our time, as a group, they faced the greatest hardships.

Once the decision has been made to create a pregnancy care ministry, the next step is prayerfully considering which members would be suitable to become "first responders" A first responder is the first point of contact and is trained to meet the physical, emotional, and spiritual needs of women and men who are facing complicated pregnancy decisions. *Making Life Disciples*, developed by Care Net, is an excellent online training resource.

After assembling and training the team, contact a local pregnancy resource center. Pregnancy resource centers would love nothing more than to establish a relationship with a church to help address the needs of those dealing with complex, unplanned pregnancies. These centers are the first point of contact for women who are considering abortion or trying to avoid it and offer the ideal partner to support your new ministry. They have highly skilled and dedicated professionals, many of whom have previously walked in their shoes and can counsel women and couples during times of crisis. Resource centers can also help with women's needs, such as diapers, car seats, strollers, etc.

The Critical Need to Promote Marriage and Responsible Fatherhood

The church is called to transform lives. Abortion is not transformational. Marriage is a transforming institution. Responsible fatherhood is transforming. Both are covenants, and covenants transform. The one who received an abortion may be surviving, not likely thriving because she came as she was and left as she was. The couple you helped remove the obstacles to birth has entered a covenant and is now thriving. They have become contributors to the church instead of remaining dependent on its services.

The importance of marriage is crucial for making abortion a redundant option in the church. It begins with recognizing a straightforward fact: almost nine out of ten abortions are among unmarried women. The decline of marriage among the group that has the most abortions (those under 34 years old), is a significant factor leading to abortion. Let's take a step back and examine why this is true and why Pro-Life people need to care deeply about marriage.

To avoid sounding clichéd, let's look at childhood. Research shows that girls who grow up without married parents are more likely to have sex and get pregnant as teens. One study found that girls without a father at home are seven times more likely to become teen mothers than girls with a father at home. This is mainly because she lacks the biological father who provides the structure and support needed to make wise decisions around relationships and sex. She is also more likely to witness an unhealthy relationship between a man and a woman.

Accordingly, before an unplanned pregnancy, a young woman's parents' marriage has a profound positive effect on her life. In the absence of this positive influence, she is more likely to experience an unplanned pregnancy as she seeks affirmation from men in less healthy places and ways. When a young woman who did not witness a healthy marriage in her household becomes pregnant outside of marriage, the lack of a strong connection with the father of her unborn child will negatively impact her decision regarding the pregnancy. Marriage is an institution designed to align the interests of mothers and fathers for the well-being of their children. We've witnessed the divorce rate increase and the marriage rate decline over the last five decades, and out-of-wedlock births and abortions have increased dramatically. Eighty-six percent of abortions occur among unmarried women, on average, because they often lack the emotional, relational, and financial support that marriage is intended to provide.

Our society has attempted to substitute marriage with cohabitation, falsely claiming that it is essentially the same as marriage but without the formalities. We know this is not true, not only that research indicates otherwise. Studies show that cohabiting relationships are more prone to violence and are generally less stable and enduring compared to marriages. It is no wonder then, that a woman in a cohabiting or any other unmarried relationship will be more likely to choose abortion over carrying her child to term.

As Pro-Life individuals, we should be deeply concerned about the state of marriage. Even after choosing life for an unborn child, there is still work to be done for both the couple and the baby. Decades of research have shown that the best environment to raise children is with their two married parents.

In the case of the couple, we don't want to see them return to the pregnancy center or abortion clinic with a new pregnancy and a new partner in another year. We must focus on helping them either build a healthy marriage with each other or, if that's not possible, work on transforming their attitudes toward marriage.

It's essential for both women and men to reconnect the concepts of sex, marriage, motherhood, and fatherhood, which have become disconnected in our culture. Even if they don't marry each other, they should make better decisions about sex and relationships for themselves and be able to pass those values on to their children.

Marriage and responsible fatherhood reduce the high abortion rates. In churches with younger congregations, a high percentage of unmarried members are more prone to unplanned pregnancies, which lead to abortion. It is the pastor who can deliver a message that helps them connect the dots of the life issue to another unplanned pregnancy (from a human perspective)—the birth of Christ. The first thing the angel told Joseph was not to be afraid to take Mary as his wife. Not your girlfriend but your wife. According to God's design, the angel affirmed the sanctity of marriage and family. God sent an angel to Joseph a second time to inform him about Jesus and the sanctity of life.

Here we see God at work preparing a basket, a safety net for the child before the child was brought into the world. Joseph and Mary were technically married, although the marriage had not been consummated. God went to great lengths to bring a savior into this world without violating his principle of first comes love, then comes marriage, and then comes the baby in the baby carriage. He set a precedent that this is how he wants children to be brought into the world.

It's certainly possible that Christ could have been born to a single mother, as it would have fulfilled God's purpose. However, it would have contradicted God's principle of marriage and family. This is why Jesus was not just given a mother, but also a father who was meant to be a husband to Mary and a father to Jesus, in that particular order. Even though Christ was fully God, God the Father understood that, in Jesus's humanity, he needed an earthly father.

God chose to give Joseph to Jesus as a reminder of the unique and irreplaceable role that husbands and fathers have in their children's lives. He then sent an angel not only to Mary but also to Joseph. Joseph was considering "putting Mary away," like many men who are facing unexpected or unexpectedly complicated pregnancies today. The angel gave Joseph the mission of being a husband and father.

Many of our women are choosing abortion because the father of the child is unable or uninterested in becoming a husband and father God intended him to be. Think how many abortions could be prevented if we had more "Josephs" stepping up to be there for today's "widows and orphans."

That is why I believe it is incumbent for the pastor to promote, support, and celebrate marriage as a critical way to reduce abortions and as the ideal environment in which children are to be raised, in God's design.

The Pro-Abundant Life movement emphasizes the importance of marriage in discouraging abortion and providing hope after a decision to terminate a pregnancy. Studies show that children raised by married parents are less likely to engage in behaviors that could lead to unplanned pregnancies, and this benefit extends into adulthood. Research also indicates that the father has the most significant influence on a woman's decision to undergo an abortion.

The woman's decision to inform the father of her unborn child about the pregnancy shows that she is expecting him to take responsibility. If she was not hoping for a positive response, she wouldn't have told him.

If someone was trying to persuade me to make a crucial decision, I would have informed them that my significant other is involved in all critical decisions, so it would be sensible for them to communicate with my partner. The crucial aspect is reaching out to the right person, which in this case is the father.

The church must adopt a similar approach to help couples considering abortion carry their pregnancy to term successfully. Perhaps the man is hesitant because he lacks confidence in his ability to be a father and husband, or he feels that he is not financially stable. All of these obstacles can be easily overcome, making abortion unnecessary.

To end abortion, ignoring the role of marriage is like trying to cure liver cancer without addressing alcoholism, the primary cause. Likewise, we must address the issue that directly contributes to abortion. While marriage is essential, we all recognize that it does not provide the best solution in all situations.

Helping parents choose life not only prevents the need for abortion but also enables couples to set an example of God's design for sex and family. It is widely acknowledged that children thrive best when raised by their own two married parents. We should celebrate the saving of a life and the formation of a family.

While it's vital to support single mothers and their children, we also need to recognize that kids in unmarried or father-absent homes often face significant challenges. It's our responsibility to offer them compassion, hope, and assistance to help them build stable and loving families. This support is crucial for mothers and fathers, giving their unborn children a better chance at a brighter future.

It's important to recognize that excluding marriage and fatherhood from discussions contributes to the problem of unwed childbearing, father absence, and the breakdown of families that we have been working to reduce for decades. Children who grow up in father-absent homes are at a higher risk of living in poverty, dropping out of school, being abused or neglected, becoming obese, being incarcerated, and becoming sexually active earlier.

As a pastor, you have the privilege of sharing with your congregants that, as fallen beings, we may fall short of God's standards and even our own. You want to make it known that you are committed to supporting both men and women who may struggle with what to do about an unplanned pregnancy.

Church members will appreciate knowing that you value them enough to address this sensitive subject by encouraging them to come to the church before making a decision they may regret later. Even though it's less than ideal circumstances, there's no condemnation.

In the Bible, although Mary's pregnancy appeared to be accidental, it wasn't, and neither is any pregnancy, whether it's expected or not. God has shown us his plan for addressing unplanned pregnancies, and he expects us to follow it. Let's lead with that and assure the woman or couple in those situations that we can trust God. He has a purpose for both the unborn baby's life and the life of the mother and the father.

CHAPTER 16

An Impassioned Plea to Pro-Life Pastors

The term "Pro-Abundant Life" was given to Care Net's president, Roland Warren, under the direction of the Holy Spirit. Roland says that the practical implications of the Pro-Abundant Life ministry are that we should focus not just on heartbeats but also on heartbeats that are heaven-bound. We should strive to ensure that every life we help bring into this world has a clear objective of reaching heaven. While it is undoubtedly the noblest of all callings to rescue a defenseless infant from the abortion gallows, as Christians, we have a unique responsibility to ensure that their "heartbeat" is aimed toward heaven and help them fulfill the plan that God has for their life. The "abundant" life—Jesus's stated purpose for coming.

In John 10:10, Jesus spoke about two different types of life. In the Greek, they are identified as Bios and Zoe. Bios refers to physical life, which is given at conception and is connected to biology. Zoe, on the other hand, is a unique spiritual life that can only be attained through a relationship with Christ. Essentially, Jesus was saying he came to link our physical life (Bios) with his spiritual life (Zoe) and enable us to become a heartbeat that's Heaven-bound. His goal was not just to give us life, but abundant life.

The Pro-Abundant Life worldview rests on two foundational pillars: marriage and family. These pillars were first established in the Garden when Adam and Eve entered a covenant relationship. Similarly, Mary and Joseph's relationship was also based on these pillars. If we imagine John 10:10 as a visual roof, we know that every roof needs at least two supports to remain stable and provide protection from the elements. The same can be said for children—they need marriage and family as God designed.

God reveals his divine design for women facing an unplanned pregnancy in the birth of Christ. Mary, a young single woman, was facing an unplanned pregnancy, which could have been overwhelming from a human perspective. I'm sure she had aspirations for her life, just like any other young woman. However, an angel came to her and announced that she would have a child. What was Mary's response? At that moment, she didn't focus on the uncertainty of what she didn't know—she focused on the one certainty she did. There's a life growing inside of me, and it's not a life to be sacrificed, but a life to be sacrificed for. So, she said, "Let it be unto me as you have said."

Consider that despite facing the probable adversities of an unplanned pregnancy, Mary's willingness to trust God by viewing her situation through the lens of her faith with, "Let it be done to me as you have said," (Luke 1:38 AMP) instead of succumbing to the Pro-Choice humanistic viewpoint.

The strategy of the Pro-Choice gospel is to overload a woman's sensory perception with everything she doesn't know: how you're going to finish your education, how you're going to raise a child on your own, how this is going to affect your relationship with the father, how is your career going to be affected, what about your parents? All the worse. I must momentarily deviate right here and inform you that every day the sun rises, pregnancy care centers across this country work with women to embrace the virtuous character of Mary, imploring them not to leave God out of their calculations.

To prevent Mary's unplanned pregnancy from becoming a crisis, God sends an angel to Joseph with the message, "do not be afraid to take Mary as your wife" (Matthew 1:20 AMPC). This highlights the sanctity of marriage and family. Before Joseph was informed about the sanctity of life, he was first told about the sanctity of marriage and family. This story reflects two sanctities or pillars—marriage and family and the sanctity of life.

God sought to create a family and a protective nest before the child was born. The Pro-Abundant Life movement follows the same blueprint that God used for his son by seeking to engage fathers. From their perspective, God's solution to Mary's unexpected pregnancy was to call Joseph to become a husband to Mary and father to their child.

The Pro-Abundant Life focus engages Mary and Joseph. God came to one man and gave him two missions: to be a husband (provider) to Mary and a father (protector) to their child.

Pro-Abundant Life's mission is to share the gospel of Jesus Christ and help people become disciples of Jesus Christ. Jesus clarified with the Great Commission, "Go and make disciples." Saving babies is not the Great Commission. Doing good "works" does not fulfill the Great Commission. Making disciples does.

The woman facing an unplanned pregnancy, the man who impregnated her, and the child growing inside of her all need to become disciples of Jesus Christ.

CHAPTER 17

Why Pro-Abundant Life

The Pro-Abundant Life approach is necessary because it's centered on the truth that lasting change is not found only in intellectually proving abortion's harm to women and their children—it is found in the person of Jesus Christ.

It has become crystal clear that despite our best efforts, the Pro-Life movement has been unsuccessful in moving the needle of compassion one degree for the protection of the "least" among us. The growing disregard for the sanctity of life has made it evident that staying on course will not lead us to where we need to be. The adage that if we keep doing what we've been doing, we'll keep getting what we've been getting has never been more applicable. At this critical juncture in our history, chart a new and better way forward. That is the Pro-Abundant Life way.

Our belief in a Creator who knew us before we were formed in the womb is central to our faith and guides our Pro-Life perspective. This holds every life as a precious gift from him, deserving protection and care from the moment of conception, and gives us the moral high ground we are still falling short.

Yes, we rightly deserve our triple A-plus rating for ministering to the needs of women and couples facing difficult pregnancy decisions and empowering them to choose life for their babies. Our ratings plummet, though, when it comes to helping them choose abundant life for their families. Overturning Roe was simply a tactic in the fight to ensure that every unborn child could have the opportunity to experience the abundant life found in Jesus Christ.

For fifty years, we've argued that abortion is the destruction of life. As ultrasound technology improved, providing even clearer pictures of babies in the womb with tiny hands, feet, and faces, as well as a beating heart, providing irrefutable evidence of life, Pro-Choice advocates dug in deeper. We had hoped these facts would move the heart of the Pro-Choice person once they realized a human life was at stake. Unfortunately, history is filled with examples of the powerful preying on the weak. Slave owners didn't deny the claim that their black slave was a person. They didn't care.

So, highlighting the humanity of the unborn child, no matter how true and important that may be, hasn't made one percentage point difference. Pregnancy center workers are no longer surprised when women see their fully formed babies on ultrasound screens and still choose to terminate their lives.

Even a study on the psychological effects of abortion published in the American Medical Archives of General Psychiatry, a study often used by the Pro-Choice community, reports that abortion results in no ill effects and that 20% of women experience regret, depression, and other emotional and psychological reactions after abortion. It has no impact. When the number of reported abortions was at its peak, almost reaching 900,000 per year, which translated into nearly 200,000 women experiencing psychological harm each year, it meant nothing. That overwhelming evidence would seem to have moved them off their Pro-Choice perch. Even our Pro-Life message of "love them both" has had zero effect. All these facts expose the shortcomings of our Pro-Life message.

The media and Pro-Choice politicians continue to promote the idea that abortion is an essential right of feminism despite efforts to counter this message. We're often accused of deceiving women when we assert that abortion negatively impacts them. The news media refuses to report the data on the psychological harm many women experience after having an abortion. They portray abortion as empowering for women, creating a misconception that being Pro-Life is anti-women. Backed up with big dollars from abortion lobbyists, our message for life doesn't fall on deaf ears; it never reaches them. As ministers of the Gospel, regardless of the constant drumbeat that abortion empowers women, we understand that the circumstances that lead to a woman's unplanned pregnancy and ensuing abortion continue after the death of her baby.

Abortion defenders often overlook the broader reality of the situation and focus solely on a woman's immediate choice to terminate her pregnancy. In doing so, they fail to consider the impact on the woman, the father of the child, and the unborn baby. They have shown no interest in helping women facing difficult pregnancy decisions with the support they need to consider the potential consequences of their choices beyond their immediate situation. Yes, abortion eliminates the baby, but not the poverty, sexual abuse, and relationship difficulties the mother faces that often lead to her being at risk of abortion. She needs to come into a transformational, life-changing relationship with Jesus Christ.

The Pro-Abundant Life focus gives us the ability to confront the realities of unplanned pregnancy and abortion head-on and refute the idea that abortion is solely a women's issue. Our Pro-Life message has proven to be too narrowly focused. We must move beyond a message that focuses exclusively on the destruction of unborn life. Instead, emphasize the holistic truth that it harms women, babies, fathers, families, and the church if we're to have a chance of turning the colossal abortion rights's ocean liner around. To do that, we begin by pointing out how the breakdown of marriage and the family over the past four decades has directly contributed to our acceptance of abortion-on-demand culture.

If our objections to abortion are solely based on its effects on the unborn or women, then we've missed the mark. Our Pro-Life services, counseling, material support, etc., alone will not break the cycle of abortion that's lurking in our pews, giving the body of Christ a black eye. As God-honoring as our Pro-Life message is, we must enlarge our mission to include raising a child and breaking the intergenerational risk of abortion.

The Pro-Life focus has been proven to save lives, but only a Pro-Abundant Life focus can transform lives. This requires encouraging couples to consider marriage and responsible fatherhood, both transforming agents. In addition, we must share the transforming message of the Gospel of Jesus Christ to empower those facing pregnancy decisions to choose life for their unborn children and abundant life for their families. Abortion rights advocates' messaging begins to fall flat to the Pro-Choice Christian when compared to this divine perspective.

The Supreme Court's legalizing abortion did severe damage to God's design for the family. It effectively separated motherhood and fatherhood while the child was still in the womb, creating incentives for some men to avoid responsibilities and for committed men to have little agency in taking responsibility for their unborn children. This lack of involvement from partners is the reason cited by the abortion-minded woman for terminating her pregnancy.

We cannot feel a sense of accomplishment that we're creating a sea of single-family homes. We should celebrate saving lives, forming a new family, and ensuring the new single mother and her child receive the support they need. However, suppose we acknowledge that children raised in father-absent homes face significant challenges in life. In that case, we might unintentionally support the flawed Pro-Choice argument that "the child would have been better off never having been born."

The only way to dismantle the narrative that abortion empowers women is to focus on promoting the Pro-Abundant Life message, emphasizing how "her body, her choice," isolates women at the worst possible time. It deprives them of the loving support they need to consider the alternatives and the full ramifications of abortion. This Pro-Abundant Life focus seeks to get upstream from the issue by addressing the reason women are becoming repeat clients of a life-affirming pregnancy help center or an abortion clinic.

The Pro-Abundant Life message, with its focus on marriage, responsible fatherhood, and discipleship, and bringing those facing unplanned pregnancies into a right relationship with Jesus Christ, is the only way to curtail this endless cycle of abortions that intensify and aggravate their lives even more. Our movement, despite its success, is unable to achieve that goal.

Being Pro-Abundant Life means saving the baby, building strong families, and breaking the intergenerational risk of abortion by creating disciples for Jesus Christ. I believe it's time we recognize the shortcomings of the past and embrace the Pro-Abundant Life movement, our best hope of moving the needle toward life and making abortion an unnecessary option in the church.

CHAPTER 18

Our "Fierce Urgency" of Now!

You may recognize that phrase from Dr. King's speech fifteen months before his assassination, imploring us to act now and seek justice with all deliberate speed. Three-quarters of a century later, we're living in another moment of the "fierce urgency of now!" It's one where we must act decisively and with great urgency to interrupt the diabolical scheme of the evil One who seeks to continually seek to destroy the image bearers of God.

For the young college student singing in the choir, terrified that her third home pregnancy test confirms what the previous two already did, presents the fierce urgency of now!

For the young minister who's just been informed his girl is pregnant and doesn't want to disappoint his parents or his pastor, thinking there's only one solution, it presents the fierce urgency of now!

For the faithful unmarried usher wrestling with the decision of whether to keep her appointment to terminate her pregnancy, it's the fierce urgency of now!

For the longtime member who has been in the church since her youth, who aborted her only child years ago, and still battles bouts of depression and finds herself at times losing her grip, it's the fierce urgency of now!

For the panicked teen who's just missed her cycle and is frantically searching the internet for black-market abortion pills, it's the fierce urgency of now!

This fierce urgency of now dramatizes the urgent need for action. There's a fierce urgency to establish pregnancy care ministries where the abortion-vulnerable can seek help before she becomes abortion-determined and apply a permanent solution to a temporary problem—one the church cannot solve. The worst advice they can receive from their Pastor is, "It's your choice." It's deadly and carries eternal weight. Instead, they need to be ministered to in a way that offers them help, hope, and compassion. This is how we begin making abortion an unnecessary option in the church. And for the ones who have yet to breach the church house doors, we must reach them with the fierce urgency of now at the pregnancy help centers. The adversity of their circumstance has softened their hearts, and they are more open to their need for a transforming relationship with Christ than ever before.

Dr. King closed his speech by saying there is such a thing as being too late. True. For too long, we've stood by in silence while the Enemy of our soul has run roughshod over the people of God. It has caused untold numbers of our sisters, our mothers, our aunts, and our grandmothers to become needlessly burdened with shame and guilt from an unnecessary abortion. Yes, it is too late for them, but it's not too late for many of those you see every Sunday. It's not too late if we follow the example of a previously unknown plow hand named Shamgar found in the book of Judges. Shamgar lamented the evil being done to his people, yet he didn't wait. "He didn't allow the moment to slip away.". He chose to act with the fierce urgency of now by starting right where he was using the tools he had and ended up slaying 600 Philistines with not much more than an oxgoad.

My prayer is that we will act with the fierce urgency of now and bring an end to this godless act of child sacrifice that's leaving a bloody stain on the bride of Christ.

NOTES

CHAPTER 7

Risk Evaluation and Mitigation Strategies (REMS), https://www.fda.gov/drugs/drug-safety-and-availability/ risk-evaluation-and-mitigation-strategies-rems.

CHAPTER 13

The Mis-Education of the Negro is a book originally published March 18, 1922 by Dr. Carter G. Woodson, page 23.

First American Birth Control Conference, held at the Hotel Plaza in New York City on November 11-12, 1921. The quote is part of a speech by Sanger and was published by the Birth Control Review, Gothic Press, on pages 172 and 174.

CHAPTER 14

The Fears Of A Birth Mother, https://www.focusonthefamily.com/Pro-Life/the-fears-of-a-birth-mother/.

The Abortion Minded Friend: How Do I Love Her In This Journey?, https://www.focusonthefamily.com/Pro-Life/the-abortion-minded-friend-how-do-i-love-her-in-this-journey/.

www.ingramcontent.com/pod-product-compliance
Lightning Source LLC
Chambersburg PA
CBHW040818120726
48005CB00012B/1456